Jesus and The Word

ALSO BY RUDOLF BULTMANN

Theology of the New Testament
Jesus Christ and Mythology

JESUS
AND
THE WORD

by RUDOLF BULTMANN

TRANSLATED BY
Louise Pettibone Smith
Erminie Huntress Lantero

Charles Scribner's Sons
New York

TRANSLATORS' PREFACE
TO THE NEW EDITION

Professor Rudolf Bultmann's *Jesus*, here translated, is a strictly historical presentation of the teaching of Jesus in the setting of the thought of his own time. Its aim is to free that teaching from certain accretions and re-interpretations, often superficial and inaccurate, which have grown up around it in modern times.

The translation of the book into English was undertaken originally in 1934 because the translators had themselves found in the book so much that was thought-provoking. It was felt by both publishers and translators that the title, *Jesus and the Word*, would convey a more definite idea of the content and viewpoint of the book than the original title, *Jesus*. This change was made with the approval of the author.

At the time when the book was first published in Germany (1926), the author was a member of a small group of continental theologians associated with Karl Barth of Switzerland. Even in 1934, he was little known in the United States. His later work, especially his writing on the need of "demythologizing" the Gospel, has been influential here as in Europe. Many Americans have sat in his class room in Marburg, and he has lectured at various educational institutions in this country.

The earlier book, however, has not lost value. The

special approach to the subject and the nature of the book itself combine to give it a less theoretical character than most of the author's work, and it has always appealed to American readers. It serves, moreover, to correct the impression sometimes gained by readers of certain of his other works—that the author is one of those who emphasize Pauline and Johannine theology at the expense of the teaching of the Jesus of the Synoptics.

Professor Bultmann's interpretation of the teaching of Jesus, however, differs radically from that popularized by liberal scholars of pre-World War One days. It forces recognition of the fact that Jesus' teaching did not center around such ideas as the infinite worth of personality, the cultivation of the inner life, the development of man toward an ideal; that Jesus spoke rather of the coming Kingdom of God, which was to be God's gift, not man's achievement, of man's decision for or against the Kingdom, and of the divine demand for obedience.

But the book is no mere return to an outworn theological traditionalism. It is of course a return to certain emphases which were prevalent throughout the history of Judaism and Christianity. Professor Bultmann recognized in the thought of the past certain essential, lasting truths which in later sophisticated times were often missed; and he has carefully and critically separated these truths from the accretions of later misinterpretations.

One of the chief stones of stumbling in the Gospels has been the eschatological element. Professor Bultmann agreed with Dr. Albert Schweitzer (cf. *The Quest of the Historical Jesus*) that eschatology was an essential part of the teaching of Jesus, but he differed from Dr. Schweitzer in his conviction that the ethical teaching of Jesus is inseparable from his eschatology : both are based on the certainty that man is not sufficient unto himself but is under the sovereignty of God. The ethic is therefore not an "interim-ethic" which has no claim on us. The eschatological interpretation of human life was not merely the teaching of a prophet nineteen centuries ago, but is essentially true today as then. Jesus' message as he delivered it, not some modern variation or dilution of it, is his message today. The details of apocalyptic imagery are transitory (here is the germ of "demythologizing"), and wishful thinking about the world to come is valueless, even harmful ; but the eschatological message, "The kingdom of God is at hand," "among you" not "within you," is relevant to any age, including our own.

Finally we suggest that no reader should allow himself to be disturbed by the purely negative element in the book. Professor Bultmann uses "know" and "certain" in an almost absolute sense ; consequently he is forced to use "probably" where most of us say "certainly," and "possibly" stands often for "probably." It is true that by his use of the methods of Form Criticism many sayings are excluded from the genuine words of Jesus. But the value of the book lies in the interpretation of Jesus' teaching as a whole, and this interpretation becomes more rather than less convincing if we ascribe to Jesus himself more of the Gospel content than Professor Bultmann is ready to do.

After twenty-five years, the translators wish again to

record their debt to Eliza Hall Kendrick, formerly Professor of Biblical History at Wellesley College, for her criticism and her help in the attempt to avoid "translation English."

LOUISE PETTIBONE SMITH

ERMINIE HUNTRESS LANTERO

SEPTEMBER, 1958

CONTENTS

ix

CONTENTS

JESUS AND THE WORD

INTRODUCTION

VIEW-POINT AND METHOD

In strict accuracy, I should not write *"view-point"*; for a fundamental presupposition of this book is that the essence of *history* cannot be grasped by "viewing" it, as we view our natural environment in order to orient ourselves in it. Our relationship to history is wholly different from our relationship to nature. Man, if he rightly understands himself, differentiates himself from nature. When he observes nature, he perceives there something objective which is not himself. When he turns his attention to history, however, he must admit himself to be a part of history; he is considering a living complex of events in which he is essentially involved. He cannot observe this complex objectively as he can observe natural phenomena; for in every word which he says about history he is saying at the same time something about himself. Hence there cannot be impersonal observation of history in the same sense that there can be impersonal observation of nature. Therefore, if this book is to be anything more than information on interesting occurrences in the past, more than a walk through a museum of antiquities, if it is really to lead to our seeing Jesus as a part of the history in which

3

we have our being, or in which by critical conflict we achieve being, then this book must be in the nature of a continuous *dialogue with history*.

Further, it should be understood that the dialogue does not come as a conclusion, as a kind of evaluation of history after one has first learned the objective facts. On the contrary, the actual encounter with history takes place only in the dialogue. We do not stand outside historical forces as neutral observers; we are ourselves moved by them; and only when we are ready to listen to the *demand* which history makes on us do we understand at all what history is about. This dialogue is no clever exercise of subjectivity on the observer's part, but a real *interrogating* of history, in the course of which the historian puts this subjectivity of his in question, and is ready to listen to history as an authority. Further, such an interrogation of history does not end in complete relativism, as if history were a spectacle wholly dependent on the individual standpoint of the observer. Precisely the contrary is true: whatever is relative to the observer—namely all the presuppositions which he brings with him out of his own epoch and training and his individual position within them—must be given up, that history may actually speak. History, however, does not speak when a man stops his ears, that is, when he assumes neutrality, but speaks only when he comes seeking answers to the questions which agitate him. Only by this attitude can we discover

4

whether an objective element is really present in history and whether history has something to say to us.

There is an approach to history which seeks by its *method* to achieve objectivity; that is, it sees history only in a perspective determined by the particular epoch or school to which the student belongs. It succeeds indeed, at its best, in escaping the subjectivity of the individual investigator, but still remains completely bound by the subjectivity of the method and is thus highly relative. Such an approach is extremely successful in dealing with that part of history which can be grasped by objective method, for example in determining the correct chronological sequence of events, and in so far forth is always indispensable. But an approach so limited misses the true significance of history. It must always question history solely on the basis of particular presuppositions, of its own method, and thus quantitatively it collects many new facts *out of* history, but learns nothing genuinely new *about* history and man. It sees in history only as little or as much of man and of humanity as it already explicitly or implicitly knows; the correctness or incorrectness of vision is always dependent on this previous knowledge.

An example may make this clear. A historian sets himself the aim of making a historical phenomenon or personality *"psychologically comprehensible."* Now this expression implies that such a writer has at his disposal complete knowledge of the psychological possibilities of life. He is therefore concerned with reducing every component of the event or of the personality to such possibilities. For that is what making anything "comprehensible" means: the reduction of it to what our previous knowledge includes. All individual facts are understood as specific cases of general laws, and these laws are assumed to be already known. On this assumption the criticism of the tradition is based, so that everything which cannot be understood on that basis is eliminated as unhistorical.

So far as purely psychological facts of the past are the objects of investigation, such a method is (for the psychological expert) quite correct. There remains, however, the question whether such a method reveals the essential of history, really brings us face to face with history. Whoever is of the belief that only through history can he find enlightenment on the contingencies of his own existence, will necessarily reject the psychological approach, however justified that method is in its own sphere. He must reject it if he is in earnest in his attempt to understand history. In such a belief this book is written. Hence no attempt is here made to render Jesus as a historical phenomenon psychologically explicable, and nothing really biographical, apart from a brief introductory section, is included.

Thus I would lead the reader not to any *"view"* of history, but to a highly personal *encounter* with history. But because the book cannot in itself be for the reader *his* encounter with history, but only information about *my* encounter with history, it does of course as a whole appear to him as a *view,* and I must define for him the point of observation. Whether he afterward remains a mere spectator is his affair.

If the following presentation cannot in the ordinary sense claim objectivity, in another sense it is all the more objective; for it refrains from *pronouncing value judgments.* The "objective" historians are often very lavish with such pronouncements, and they thus introduce a subjective element which seems to me unjustified. Purely formal evaluations of the meaning of an event or a person in the immediate historical sequence are of course necessary; but a *judgment of value* depends upon a point of view which the writer imports into the history and by which he measures the historical phenomena. Obviously the criticisms which many historians deliver, favorable or unfavorable, are given from a standpoint beyond history. As against this I have especially aimed to avoid everything beyond history and to find a position for myself *within* history. Therefore evaluations which depend on the distinction between the historical and the super-historical find no place here.

Indeed, if one understands by the historical process only phenomena and incidents determinable in time—"what happened"—then he has occasion to look for something beyond the historical fact which can motivate the interest in history. But then the suspicion becomes most insistent that the essential of history has been missed; for the essential of history is in reality nothing *super*-historical, but is event in time. Accordingly this book lacks all the phraseology which speaks of Jesus as great man, genius, or hero; he appears neither as inspired nor as inspiring,[1] his sayings are not called profound, nor his faith mighty, nor his nature child-like. There is also no consideration of the eternal values of his message, of his discovery of the infinite depths of the human soul, or the like. Attention is entirely limited to what he *purposed,* and hence to what in his purpose as a part of history makes a present demand on us.

For the same reason, *interest in the personality of Jesus* is excluded—and not merely because, in the absence of information, I am making a virtue of necessity. I do indeed think that we can now know almost nothing concerning the life and personality of Jesus, since the early Christian sources show no interest in either, are moreover fragmentary and often legendary; and other sources about Jesus do not exist. Except for the purely critical research, what has been written in the last hundred and fifty years on the life of Jesus, his personality and the development of his inner life, is fantastic and romantic. Whoever reads Álbert Schweitzer's brilliantly written *Quest of the Historical Jesus*[2] must vividly realize this. The same impression is made by a survey

[1] Literally, "neither as dæmonic nor as fascinating."
[2] Translated by W. Montgomery. London, 1910.

of the differing contemporary judgments on the question of the Messianic consciousness of Jesus, the varying opinions as to whether Jesus believed himself to be the Messiah or not, and if so, in what sense, and at what point in his life. Considering that it was really no trifle to believe oneself Messiah, that, further, whoever so believed must have regulated his whole life in accordance with this belief, we must admit that if this point is obscure we can, strictly speaking, know nothing of the personality of Jesus. I am personally of the opinion that Jesus did not believe himself to be the Messiah, but I do not imagine that this opinion gives me a clearer picture of his personality. I have in this book not dealt with the question at all—not so much because nothing can be said about it with certainty as because I consider it of secondary importance.

However good the reasons for being interested in the personalities of significant historical figures, Plato or Jesus, Dante or Luther, Napoleon or Goethe, it still remains true that this interest does not touch that which such men had at heart; for *their* interest was not in their personality but in their *work*. And their work was to them not the expression of their personality, nor something through which their personality achieved its "form," but the cause to which they surrendered their lives. Moreover, their work does not mean the sum of the historical effects of their acts; for to this their view could not be directed. Rather, the "work" from *their*

9

standpoint is the end they really sought, and it is in connection with their purpose that they are the proper objects of historical investigation. This is certainly true if the examination of history is no neutral orientation about objectively determined past events, but is motivated by the question how we ourselves, standing in the current of history, can succeed in comprehending our own existence, can gain clear insight into the contingencies and necessities of our own life purpose.

In the case of those who like Jesus have worked through the medium of *word,* what they purposed can be reproduced only as a group of sayings, of ideas—as *teaching.* Whoever tries, according to the modern fashion, to penetrate behind the teaching to the psychology or to the personality of Jesus, inevitably, for the reasons already given, misses what Jesus purposed. For his purpose can be comprehended only as teaching.

But in studying the teaching there is again danger of misunderstanding, of supposing such teaching to be a system of general truths, a system of propositions which have validity apart from the concrete life situation of the speaker. In that case it would follow that the truth of such statements would necessarily be measured by an ideal universal system of truths, of eternally valid propositions. In so far as the thought of Jesus agreed with this ideal system, one could speak of the super-historical element in his message. But here it would again become clear that one has missed the essential of history, has not met with anything really new in history. For this ideal system would not be learned from history, it implies rather a standard beyond history by which the particular historical phenomena are measured. The study of history would then at best consist in bringing this pre-existent ideal system to clearer recognition through the observation of concrete "cases." Historical research would be a work of "recollection" in the Platonic sense, a clarifying of knowledge which man already possesses. Such a view would be essentially rationalistic; history as event in time would be excluded.

Therefore, when I speak of the teaching or thought of Jesus, I base the discussion on no underlying conception of a universally valid system of thought which through this study can be made enlightening to all. Rather the ideas are understood in the light of the concrete situation of a man living in time; as his interpretation of his own existence in the midst of change, uncertainty, decision; as the expression of a possibility of comprehending this life; as the effort to gain clear insight into the contingencies and necessities of his own existence. When we encounter the words of Jesus in history, *we* do not judge *them* by a philosophical system with reference to their rational validity; *they* meet *us* with the question of how we are to interpret our own existence. That we be ourselves deeply disturbed by the problem of our own life is therefore the indispensable condition of our inquiry. Then the examination of history will lead not to the enrichment of timeless wisdom, but to an encounter with history which itself is an event in time. This is dialogue with history.

There is little more to say in introduction. The subject of this book is, as I have said, not the life or the personality of Jesus, but only his teaching, his message. Little as we know of his life and personality, we know enough of his *message* to make for ourselves a consistent picture. Here, too, great caution is demanded by the nature of our sources. What the sources offer us is first of all the message of the early Christian community, which for the most part the church freely attributed to Jesus. This naturally gives no proof that all the words which are put into his mouth were actually spoken by him. As can be easily proved, many sayings originated in the church itself; others were modified by the church.

Critical investigation shows that the whole tradition about Jesus which appears in the three synoptic gospels is composed of a series of layers which can on the whole be clearly distinguished, although the separation at some points is difficult and doubtful. (The Gospel of John cannot be taken into account at all as a source for the teaching of Jesus, and it is not referred to in this book.) The separating of these layers in the synoptic gospels depends on the knowledge that these gospels were composed in Greek within the Hellenistic Christian community, while Jesus and the oldest Christian group lived in Palestine and spoke Aramaic. Hence everything in the synoptics which for reasons of language or content can have originated only in Hellenistic Christianity must be excluded as a source for the teaching of Jesus. The critical analysis shows, however, that the essential content of these three gospels was taken over from the Aramaic tradition of the oldest Palestinian community. Within this Palestinian material again different layers can be distinguished, in which whatever betrays the specific interests of the church or reveals characteristics of later development must be rejected as secondary. By means of this critical analysis an oldest layer is determined, though it can be marked off with only relative exactness. Naturally we have no absolute assurance that the exact words of this oldest layer were really spoken by Jesus. There is a possibility that the contents of this oldest layer are also the result of a complicated historical process which we can no longer trace.

Of course the doubt as to whether Jesus really existed is unfounded and not worth refutation. No sane person can doubt that Jesus stands as founder behind the historical movement whose first distinct stage is represented by the oldest Palestinian community. But how far that community preserved an objectively true picture of him and his message is another question. For those whose interest is in the personality of Jesus, this situation is depressing or destructive; for our purpose it has no particular significance. It is precisely this complex of ideas in the oldest layer of the synoptic tradition which is the object of our consideration. It meets us as a fragment of tradition coming to us from the past, and in the examination of it we seek the encounter with history. By the tradition Jesus is named as bearer of the message; according to overwhelming probability he really was. Should it prove otherwise, that does not change in any way what is said in the record. I see then no objection to naming Jesus throughout as the speaker. Whoever prefers to put the name of "Jesus" always in quotation marks and let it stand as an abbreviation for the historical phenomenon with which we are concerned, is free to do so. Further I need say only that I have in what follows seldom given the critical considerations; they can be found in their context in my book *Die Geschichte der synoptischen Tradition*[1] in connection with my own critical analysis.

After a historical introduction, this presentation of the message of Jesus is developed in three concentric circles of thought. In each circle we are concerned with the same question; but this common centre can first be clearly recognized only in the smallest circle. The smallest circle is, however, comprehensible only when one has passed through the two outer circles.

Finally I wish to say that this book does not deal with especially complicated or difficult matters, but with

[1] Göttingen, Vanderhoeck and Ruprecht, 2d ed., 1931.

extremely simple ones, so far as theoretical understanding is concerned. Of course the understanding of simple things can be difficult, but such difficulty is due not to the nature of the things but to the fact that we have forgotten how to see directly, being too much burdened with presuppositions. This is so characteristic of our contemporary situation that the following discussion may appear difficult simply because it is trying to gain for the author as well as for the reader the right method of seeing. If I am wrong in anticipating difficulty, so much the better; but the reader should realize that no end is gained by making the matter seem easier than it really is, in relation to the intellectual attitude of the present day. The essential difficulty in this book, however, lies not in the theoretical understanding nor in the acceptance of it as a "point of view," but in the actual encounter with reality which it demands. Now for a great end one must be ready to pay the price, and I would rather frighten a reader away than attract one who wants something for nothing.

I

The Historical Background for the Ministry of Jesus

1. The Jewish Religion

A unique picture is presented by the Jewish nation as it existed at the beginning of our era, with its centre in Jerusalem, the holy city. This nation, through a varied history, rich in external and internal experience, had become far removed from the primitive life of immediate dependence on nature, in which neighboring Oriental peoples still more or less lingered. It was a nation whose political life had been finally destroyed by the Roman rule, and whose economic situation involved no problems the solution of which could affect historical development. A people, furthermore, which had no intellectual or spiritual life in the sense of cultural achievements such as science, art, or jurisprudence, developed for their own sake. A people endowed with great vitality, strong natural instincts, the highest moral energy, and the keenest intellectual capacity, yet whose life consisted not in all the things which fill the life of the other peoples of the earth.

Law and *promise* determine the life of this people,

obedience and *hope* define its meaning. *Law*—not a law arising from the concrete relationships of life, based upon rational thinking and logically articulated; on the contrary, a law which had grown out of social conditions and cultic motives no longer alive and often no longer understood, artificially preserved and casuistically elaborated and interpreted. A law not lacking a strong infusion of ethical ideas, yet not to be characterized as a "moral code." A law which does not rest upon the ethical conception of man and humanity, but which is characterized by a combination of ethical and legalistic viewpoints. A law which properly has only this meaning: to release man from the world, to separate him from any interest in an independent cultural development, and to humble him in obedience to the transcendent power of God—of a *God,* whose image is not in any sense determined by the conception that man has of his own highest spiritual life. A God who at first glance is comparable to the picture of the Oriental ruler, who governs his people with complete arbitrariness, bound by no rational law; but a God who is conceived as wholly different from an Oriental ruler, since all physical traits are lacking, all tyrannical desires alien; a God who desires justice and righteousness and punishes sin, a God who loves His people as a father his first-born son, a God to whom the religious man calls as to his father, and in whose help he trusts in all situations of life.

This law and the unconditional obedience of the religious man to it make the Jewish nation a *chosen* people. The primary sense of this title—irrespective of what arrogant or naïvely material claims may be combined with it—is that this people is a holy people; it is lifted out of the world, out of the world's interests and ideals, and has its centre of gravity in the beyond. Exactly the same meaning underlies also *promise* and *hope*. For the hope has as its content not some kind of program for a political, judicial, or economic ideal. Israel hoped not for an ideal world order (if the word "ideal" be used in its strict sense), but for the end of earthly things and for the glory of God and His people. And although naïve imagination could represent this glory only in pictures which betray pleasure in material splendor and sensuous enjoyments, still this is not the essential element.

In reality such descriptions have only the negative significance that in the promised day all the misery of life, its poverty and sickness, will end; the foreign rule of the heathen will be over. But of what then will positively be, there is no definite picture. There is only the assurance that the holy God will dwell in the midst of His holy people. Such hope rests on the promise of the prophets, whose relation to earlier concrete historical situations is ignored. The prophets themselves were already saturated with Oriental mythology; and the later hope of Judaism was also deeply influenced by the my-

thology of Oriental eschatologies, of Persian or Babylon-
ian origin. The result was a new and peculiar literary
form, apocalyptic, which sought to unravel the secrets
of the divine plan for the world, to recognize the signs
of the end, to calculate the time of its arrival, and to in-
vent fantastic elaborations of the heavenly glory.

Hope is peculiarly bound up with *obedience;* they
support each other. In rabbinical Judaism after the beginning of the Christian era the hope retreats more and
more into the background, not indeed as a fundamental
conception but as a practical attitude. Rabbinical Judaism finally rejected apocalyptic, leaving it to Christianity, and concentrated entirely on the Law. How far
this movement had gone among the rabbis in the time
of Jesus, it is difficult to say. At any rate *the Jewish
people at just this time were most strongly stirred by
Messianic hopes.* These hopes were depicted in a great
variety of colors, depending on whether the traditional
picture of the old Davidic kingdom or fantastic Oriental cosmology and mythology made the greater con-
tribution; on whether political ideals determined their
thoughts, or a purely religious hope predominated.

Because of the close connection between obedience
and hope, *one* particular expectation especially filled
many minds: the hope that God would destroy the rule
of the heathen, that He would again make of Palestine
a completely holy land in which only the law of their
fathers would prevail. It is true that the official class

of the Jewish people welcomed the Roman rule, which gave peace to the land and, in the very act of depriving the race of its national existence, allowed the religious man to work in peace and live faithful to the Law. In the temple at Jerusalem, too, sacrifices and prayers were offered regularly for the Cæsar, and Jewish leaders were satisfied so long as the Romans showed a certain consideration for the holiness of Jerusalem. But among the people themselves, and especially in the strictly legalistic group, the Pharisees, there grew out of the Messianic hope a flaming activism, which itself undertook to end the rule of the heathen. From the time of Herod the Great the *Messianic movements* did not cease, until they finally culminated in the destruction of Jerusalem and the annihilation of the Jewish state—in so far as it could be called a state.

2. *The Messianic Movements*

Herod had already had to use force to suppress a conspiracy which had begun when he had aroused religious antagonism by setting up trophies in the theatre at Jerusalem. As he lay on his deathbed, Jewish youths tore down and destroyed the golden eagle which he had brought into the temple. At the beginning of the reign of Archelaus, to avenge the execution of these offenders, there was a revolt at the feast of the Passover; it was put down by violence. Similarly after the death of Herod an insurrection broke out in Galilee under a certain Judas; it was merely the continuation of earlier disturbances with which Herod had had to deal. In Perea a certain Simon proclaimed himself "king." In Judea a brawny shepherd assumed a crown and began war against the Romans and Herodians. The Jewish historian Josephus calls the rebels "bandits"; the context shows however that without exception these were Messianic movements. When in 6 A.D. the Syrian legate Quirinius took a census in Palestine, there was a revolt in Galilee, and the Judas before mentioned together with the Pharisee Zadok founded the party of the Zealots; religiously the Zealots belonged with the Pharisees, but they made their Messianic hope into a political program. They considered it shameful to pay tribute to the Romans, and to endure mortal men as lords instead of God, the only Lord and King. As they accepted willingly for themselves any kind of death, so also was the murder of relatives and friends a matter of indifference to them, if only they need not call any man their lord. Until the fall of Jerusalem these Zealots continued to defy the Romans, and with them were the like-minded Sicarii, who did not shrink even from the murder of the high priest. Pilate had to suppress in Judea two smaller uprisings, called forth by the offending of Jewish religious feeling; in Samaria he was forced to resort to bloodshed in order to put down a Messianic revolt.

After 40 A.D. such movements multiplied. The old

unrest continued. Here and there in Jerusalem and in the country insurrections occurred. Here and there Messianic prophets and even "kings" appeared; under Cuspius Fadus, the "prophet" Theudas; under Ventidius Cumanus, the "bandit" Eleasar; under Felix, a "prophet" who came out of Egypt, who led the crowd of his adherents to the Mount of Olives and attempted to enter Jerusalem with them, expecting the walls to fall at his command; under Festus, a "prophet" who promised "salvation" and deliverance from all suffering. In fact, there was a whole succession of prophets who, according to the account of Josephus, "behaving as if they were chosen by God, caused disturbances and revolutions and drove the people insane with their oratory, and enticed them into the desert, as if God might there announce to them the miracle of their deliverance." All these Messianic insurrections the Romans suppressed and crucified their instigators or executed them in other ways whenever they could get their hands on them. Here it must be emphasized that some of these movements had no political character. The crowds stirred with Messianic hopes often used no violence, but expected the end of the Roman rule and the coming of the Kingdom of God to be achieved purely by a miracle of God's working. The Romans did not distinguish, and indeed they could not; for them, all these movements were suspected as hostile to the Roman authority.

3. John the Baptist and Jesus

At this time a prophet appeared by the Jordan, John the Baptist. His coming, too, belongs in the series of Messianic movements. It had of course no political character, but it was inspired by the certainty that the time of the end was now come. On the ground of this conviction he preached repentance.

"You brood of vipers! Who has taught you to flee from the wrath to come? Bring forth then fit fruits of repentance, and think not to say within yourselves: We have Abraham for our father. For I tell you, God can raise up from these stones children to Abraham. Already the axe is laid at the root of the trees, and every tree which does not bear fruit is cut down and thrown into the fire!" (Matt. 3:7–10)

He came as an ascetic, and fasting was characteristic of his sect. (Mark 2:18, Matt. 11:18) In addition he practised *baptism*. Judaism, like the other religions of the east, had long practised the washings which were intended to preserve cultic and ritual purity. At the time of the rise of Christianity, however, there had appeared in that part of the world a whole group of baptismal sects, to which for example the so-called Essenes belong. There was a special significance ascribed to baptism, which was obviously connected with eschatological speculations. Hence the baptism which John proclaimed must be understood as an eschatological sacrament.

Whoever submitted himself to it, and to the obligation of repentance bound up with it, purified himself for the coming Kingdom of God, and belonged to the company of those who would escape the day of wrath and judgment. Clearly ancient eastern, non-Jewish conceptions influenced this Baptist movement; old mythology of Persia or Babylon perhaps also influenced the Baptist's preaching of the coming Judge. But we know little about it from the earliest sources—the gospel and Josephus. Possibly the Mandæan Gnostic sect which emerged later is a development of this old Baptist sect, and perhaps many of the Mandæan conceptions go back to the beginning of the movement. It is worth noting that the Mandæans called themselves "Nazarenes"; and that Jesus is often so called in the early Christian tradition. Since this epithet cannot be derived from the name of his own village Nazareth, and since the early Christian tradition has preserved the recollection that Jesus was baptized by John, it might be concluded that Jesus originally belonged to the sect of the Baptist, and that the Jesus-sect was an offshoot of the John-sect. To this conclusion other traces in the gospel tradition point, sayings which stress now the agreement between Jesus and the Baptist, now the superiority of Jesus over John; sayings which show now the solidarity of the two sects as against orthodox Judaism, now the rivalry between them.

But this matter must not be further discussed here. The important point is that among the many Messianic movements of the time, in close relation to the sect of the Baptizer, that movement also grew up which Jesus initiated by his preaching. His followers saw in Jesus the Messiah, whose return after his execution they expected. (We know of something similar in the case of a Samaritan sect.) *Both movements, that of John and that of Jesus, were Messianic.* Their connection with each other and also with other Messianic movements is recognizable in the fact that disciples of the Baptist came over to Jesus, and that there was even a Zealot among Jesus' followers.

Outsiders certainly could not recognize the essentially unpolitical character of the leadership of both John and Jesus, especially as both aroused considerable popular excitement. Both movements were therefore suppressed quickly by the execution of their leaders. John the Baptist was beheaded by Herod Antipas. Mark 6:17–29 gives us an entirely legendary account of his death, while Josephus states that Herod, in view of the crowds which flocked to the Baptist, was afraid that John would incite the people to rebellion, and prevented this by executing him. Jesus was crucified by the Roman procurator Pontius Pilate. What rôle the Jewish authorities, on whom the Christian tradition put the chief blame, actually played is no longer clearly discernible. It is probable that they, as in other cases, worked hand in hand with the Romans in the interest of political tranquillity. At least there can be no doubt that Jesus like other agitators died on the cross as a Messianic prophet.

II

THE TEACHING OF JESUS: THE COMING OF THE KINGDOM OF GOD

1. The Proclamation of Deliverance[1] and Call to Repentance

The message of Jesus is an *eschatological gospel*—the proclamation that now the fulfillment of the promise is at hand, that now the Kingdom of God begins:

"Happy are the eyes that see what you see! for I tell you: Many prophets and kings have desired to see what you see, and have not seen it; to hear what you hear, and have not heard it." (Luke 10:23, 24)

Then the summons to deliverance rings out:

"Happy are you poor, for yours is the Kingdom of God, Happy are you who hunger now, for you shall be filled, Happy are you who weep now, for you shall laugh."
(Luke 6:20, 21)

If the Kingdom of God is beginning, then the rule of Satan, who now with his evil demons infests the earth, must be ending. And indeed the demons can be seen already in flight; their cause is lost. Jesus and his

[1] *Heil* has a somewhat broader meaning than any one English equivalent. The translation "deliverance" has usually been chosen rather than "salvation," in accordance with the emphasis of the crisis theologians that Christian salvation is not a possession.

disciples in the consciousness of their mission drive out demons and heal the sick. A strange word of Jesus to his disciples is recorded:

"I saw Satan fall like lightning from heaven. Behold, I give you power to tread on serpents and scorpions and over all the might of the enemy, and nothing shall by any means harm you " (Luke 10:18,19)

He answers the doubters:

"If I by the finger of God drive out the demons, then the Kingdom of God has come to you." (Luke 11:20)

He who has eyes to see must recognize that God, the stronger, has triumphed over Satan and broken his power; for

"No one can enter the house of a strong man and plunder it, unless he has first bound the strong man." (Mark 3:27)

It is true then! The promise of the prophets is fulfilled.

"The blind see, and the lame walk,
The lepers are cleansed, and the deaf hear,
The dead are raised, and the poor have the gospel
    preached to them." (Matt. 11:5)

The time of joy begins: mourning and fasting are past; it is festival time—and who may fast during the days of the marriage feast? (Mark 2:19)

However little we know of the life of Jesus, if we keep in mind that he was finally crucified as a Messianic agitator, we shall be able in the light of the eschatological message to understand the fragmentary accounts of the end of his activity, overgrown though they are with legend. He seems to have entered Jerusalem with a crowd of enthusiastic adherents; all were full of joy and of confidence that now the Kingdom of God was beginning. It was a band like that which the Egyptian prophet attempted to lead to Jerusalem, which was halted and scattered by a division of troops sent by the Procurator Felix to meet it. Jesus entered Jerusalem, and with his followers took possession (as it seems) of the temple, in order to cleanse the holy precincts from all evil in preparation for the coming of the Kingdom.

The oldest account of the last meal of Jesus with his disciples (Luke 22:15–18) contains a significant saying:

"With desire I have desired to eat this passover with
    you before I suffer.
for I tell you:
I will not any more eat of it until it be eaten in the
    Kingdom of God.
And he took the cup, and gave thanks, and said:
Take this and divide it among yourselves.
for I tell you:
I will not drink of the fruit of the vine
until the Kingdom of God is come."

Even this account has a legendary coloring; but possibly it preserves an old saying in which Jesus affirmed the certainty that he would celebrate the next (Passover?) feast with his followers in the Kingdom of God.

At any rate his message is based on the certainty: *the Kingdom of God is beginning, is beginning now!* His own activity is for him and for his followers the sign that the Kingdom is imminent. It is absurd and presumptuous to ask him for a specific sign as evidence (Mark 8:11, 12); his message accredits him. The cleverness of the men of this world is foolishness, since they know, when the fig tree begins to grow green, that summer is coming; they can interpret the signs of sky, clouds, and wind, to predict the weather; but they do not understand the signs of the present age and do not know that it is the last hour. (Mark 13:28, 29; Luke 12:54–56)

In this last hour, the hour of decision, Jesus is sent with the final, decisive word. Happy is he who understands it and is not offended in him! (Matt. 11:6) Decision is inevitable—for him or against him: "He who is not with me is against me, and he who does not gather with me, scatters." (Matt. 12:30) Wiser was the queen of Sheba, who of old came to Solomon to hear his wisdom; wiser were the Ninevites, who repented at the preaching of the prophet Jonah—wiser than the fools of this generation, who do not understand what is happening before their eyes. (Luke 11:31, 32) But soon, when the Kingdom of God comes, when the Judge of the world, the "Son of Man" appears, Jesus will be justified and:

"Whoever acknowledges me before men,

him the Son of Man will also acknowledge before the
  angels of God.
He who denies me before men
shall be denied before the angels of God."
                                        (Luke 12 :8, 9)

Now is the time of decision: "Follow me and let the
dead bury their dead." (Matt. 8 :22) "No man who
puts his hand to the plow and looks back is fit for the
Kingdom of God." (Luke 9 :62)

"For the sake of the Kingdom of God" involves complete renunciation, brings every man face to face with
the ultimate *Either-Or*.[1] To decide for the Kingdom is
to sacrifice for it all things else.

"The Kingdom of God is like a treasure hidden in a
field, which a man found and hid, and in his joy he
went and sold all that he had, and bought the field.
"The Kingdom of God is like a merchant seeking
goodly pearls, who when he found a pearl of great price
went and sold all that he had, and bought the pearl."
(Matt. 13 :44–46)

"If your eye leads you astray, pluck it out and cast
it from you. For it is better that one of your members
perish, than that your whole body should be cast into
hell.
"If your hand leads you astray, cut it off and cast it
from you. For it is better that one of your members
perish, than that your whole body should go into hell."
(Matt. 5 :29, 30)

[1] *Entweder-Oder:* a phrase of Kierkegaard often used by the
crisis theologians.

31

There are people who for the Kingdom's sake have made themselves eunuchs, says Jesus. (Matt. 19:12) The road to deliverance leads through the narrow gate only; the many on the broad way are travelling to destruction. (Matt. 7:13, 14) This call to decision is the call to *repentance*. For most men cling to this world, and do not muster energy to decide wholly for God. They do desire the Kingdom, but they desire it along with other things—riches, and the respect of other men; they are not ready for repentance. When the invitation to the Kingdom comes to them they are claimed by various other interests.

"A man prepared a great supper and invited many. And he sent his servant at supper-time to call those who were invited: Come, for now it is ready. And they all began with one accord to excuse themselves. The first said: I have bought a field and must go out and see it; I beg you to excuse me. And another said: I have bought five yoke of oxen and I am going to try them; I beg you to excuse me. And another said: I have married a wife and therefore I cannot come. And the servant came and told his master these things.

"Then the master of the house became angry and said to the servant: Go out quickly into the streets and lanes of the city, and bring in the poor and maimed and blind and lame. And the servant said: Master, what you commanded is done, and yet there is room. Then said the master to the servant: Go out into the highways and the hedges and compel them to come in, that my house may be filled. For I tell you, not one of those men who were invited shall taste of my supper." (Luke 14:16–24)

The call to the Kingdom of God is accordingly, as the parable shows, an invitation which is at the same time a demand. Those who are invited must put the Kingdom of God above all other things. It makes its claim not on man's frivolous desire for pleasure but on his will. The word of invitation is at the same time a word of warning:

"Who of you when he intends to build a tower does not first sit down and count the cost, whether he has enough to complete it? Otherwise when he has laid a foundation and is not able to finish, all that see it begin to mock him, saying, This man began to build and was not able to finish.

"Or what king, as he goes to encounter another king in war, does not first sit down and consult whether with ten thousand he is able to meet him who comes against him with twenty thousand? If not, he sends him an embassy while he is still far away and asks for terms of peace." (Luke 14:28–32)

A man therefore should think seriously before he decides to have anything to do with this invitation. A ready acceptance in words has no value; an act of will is required.

"Why do you call me Lord, Lord, and do not do what I say? Everyone who comes to me and hears my words and does them, I will show you whom he is like. He is like a man who built a house, who dug deep and laid a foundation upon a rock. Then when the flood came, the stream broke upon that house but could not shake it, because it was founded upon a rock. But he who hears and does not is like a man who built a house upon the earth without a foundation. When the stream broke against it, it fell immediately, and the ruin of that house was great." (Luke 6:46–49)

How far must devotion and readiness for self-sacrifice be carried?

"If any man comes to me and does not hate father and mother, wife and children, brothers and sisters, yes, and his own life also, he cannot be my disciple." (Luke 14:26)

In two brief narratives belonging to the later stratum of the tradition, the church has shown vividly how this decisive Either-Or dominates the preaching of Jesus, how every other interest disappears before the exclusiveness of the demand of God.

"It happened, as Jesus was speaking, that a woman of the people raised her voice and said: Happy is the womb which bore you and the breast which gave you suck! But he said: Rather, happy are they who hear the word of God and keep it." (Luke 11:27–28)

"And there came his mother and his brothers, and standing outside they sent to call him, for a crowd was sitting around him. And they told him, Your mother and your brothers outside are looking for you. And he answered: Who are my mother and my brothers? And looking at those who were sitting around him, he said: See, here are my mother and my brothers! Whoever does the will of God is my brother and sister and mother." (Mark 3:31–35)

34

2. The Kingdom of God

What then is the meaning of "the Kingdom of God?" How is it to be conceived? The simplest answer is: the Kingdom of God is deliverance for men. It is that *eschatological* deliverance which ends everything earthly. This deliverance is the only deliverance which can properly be so called; therefore it demands of man decision. It is not something which man can possess along with other good things, which he may pursue along with other interests. This deliverance confronts man as an Either-Or.

To 150

Thus it is meaningless to call the Kingdom of God the "highest value," if by this is meant the culmination of all that men consider good. And the phrase would still not express truly the distance between the Kingdom of God and all other values, even if the relativity of these other values to this highest value is emphasized. A "highest value" always remains in connection with the relative. The Kingdom of God as eschatological deliverance is diametrically opposed to all relative values —provided that the idea of eschatology is wholly and radically understood; and such an understanding must now be sought.

It is already clear that the Kingdom of God is *no "highest good" in the ethical sense.* It is not a good toward which the will and action of men is directed, not an ideal which is in any sense realized through human

35

conduct, which in any sense requires *men* to bring it into existence. Being eschatological, it is wholly supernatural. Against all impatience which would bring in the Kingdom by force, the parable speaks:

"The Kingdom of God is as if a man throws seed on the land. He sleeps and rises up, as day follows night, and the seed sprouts and grows up, he knows not how. The earth brings forth fruit of itself, first the blade, then the ear, then the ripe grain in the ear. When the grain is ripe, he sends the reapers, for the harvest is ready." (Mark 4:26–29)

Such a parable must not be read in the light of the modern conceptions of "nature" and "evolution." The parable presupposes that the growth and ripening of the seed is not something "natural," within man's control, but that it is something miraculous. As the grain springs up miraculously and ripens without human agency or understanding, so marvellous is the coming of the Kingdom of God. If we need proof that we must lay aside our modern view-point in order to understand such a saying in the sense of primitive Christianity, let us consider a very similar parable of the early Christian tradition. It is found in the first Epistle of Clement, dating from the end of the first century, and there the interpretation is given. The parable is to show how inevitably the divine judgment comes.

"O you fools, consider a plant, a grapevine for example. First it sheds the old leaves, then the young shoots sprout, then leaves, then flowers, then the green grapes, finally the ripe grapes appear. You see how quickly the fruit is ripe. Even so quickly and suddenly will God's final judgment come, as the Scripture testifies: He will come quickly and will not tarry, suddenly the Lord will come to His temple, the Holy One for whom you wait." (I Clem. 23:4, 5)

The Kingdom of God, then, is something miraculous, in fact the absolute miracle, opposed to all the here and now; it is "wholly other," heavenly (*cf*. R. Otto). Whoever seeks it must realize that he cuts himself off from the world, otherwise he belongs to those who are not fit, who put their hand to the plow and look back. The stories of the calling of the first disciples are legends (Mark 1:16–20, 2:14); he who seeks for a historical kernel in them by attempting to explain psychologically the behavior of the disciples misunderstands them. But these legends are the historical witness for the meaning of Jesus' message concerning the Kingdom, which tears men up by the roots from their business life and from their social relationships and commands the dead to bury their dead. "The saints," the company of disciples of Jesus soon called themselves—those who are separated from the present world and have their life in the beyond.

Although the metaphor of "entering into" the Kingdom of God often occurs that does not imply any possibility of conceiving the Kingdom as something which either is or can be realized in any organization of world fellowship. Naturally both the Greek word and the Aramaic behind it can be translated as "Realm of God."

However, this translation is a dangerous one, for all modern conceptions of citizens or members of the state, of fellow-countrymen and the like, are utterly mistaken. The Kingdom of God is not an ideal which realizes itself in human history; we cannot speak of its founding, its building, its completion; we can say only that it draws near, it comes, it appears. It is *supernatural, superhistorical;* and while men can "receive" its salvation, can enter it, it is not *they,* with their fellowship and their activity, who constitute the Kingdom, but God's power alone. Even if the parables of the mustard-seed and the leaven really applied originally to the Kingdom of God, they were certainly not intended to denote the "natural" growth of the Kingdom, but were meant to show how inescapable will be its coming, however easily ignored or misinterpreted may be the signs of its coming which are conspicuous in the activity of Jesus. The marvellous, superhistorical character of the Kingdom is the constant presupposition.

But must we stop at this merely negative definition? What should we understand positively by the Kingdom of God? What sort of *events* are meant when its coming is announced? There can be no doubt that Jesus like his contemporaries expected a tremendous eschatological drama. Then will the "Son of Man" come, that heavenly Messianic figure, which appeared in the apocalyptic hope of later Judaism, partly obliterating the older Messianic figure of the Davidic king and partly combining with it. Then will the dead rise, the judgment will take place, and to some the heavenly glory will be revealed while others will be cast into the flames of hell, where there will be weeping and gnashing of teeth. Evidently Jesus shared with his contemporaries the belief in all these dramatic events. As in that saying at the last supper, so at other times too, he speaks with entire naturalness of eating and drinking in the Kingdom of God.

But it should be noted that he neither depicts the punishments of hell nor paints elaborate pictures of the heavenly glory. The oracular and esoteric note is completely lacking in the few prophecies of the future which can be ascribed to him with any probability. In fact he absolutely repudiates all representations of the Kingdom which human imagination can create, when he says:

"When they rise from the dead, they neither marry nor are given in marriage, but are as the angels in heaven." (Mark 12:25)

In other words, men are forbidden to make any picture of the future life. Jesus thus *rejects the whole content of apocalyptic speculation,* as he rejects also the calculation of the time and the watching for signs. It is said for example in a Jewish apocalypse:

"If the Almighty spare your life, then after three times
        you will see the land in confusion.
Then suddenly the sun will shine by night
and the moon by day.

From the trees will drip blood,
stones will dry out.
The nations will fall into tumult,
the heavenly regions into chaos;
and there shall come to power one whom dwellers on
    earth expect not.
The birds fly away,
the sea of Sodom brings forth fish,
and roars at night with a voice, which many do not un-
    derstand, though all hear.
At many places the abyss opens,
fire bursts forth and blazes long,
then the wild beasts forsake their haunts.
Women bear monsters,
in fresh water salt is found. . . ." (4 Ezra 6:4–9)

In the teaching of Jesus nothing of this kind is found,
rather the warning against all such calculation:

"The Kingdom of God does not so come that the time
of its coming can be calculated; none can say, Look
here, or Look there, for see, the Kingdom of God is
(suddenly) in your midst." (Luke 17:20, 21)

"And if someone says to you, Look here, or Look
there, do not go running hither and yon. For as the
lightning flashes and shines from one end of the heavens
to the other, so will the Son of Man be in his day."
(Luke 17:23, 24)

The real significance of "the Kingdom of God" for
the message of Jesus does not in any sense depend on
the dramatic events attending its coming, nor on any
circumstances which the imagination can conceive. It
interests him not at all as a describable state of existence,

but rather as the transcendent event, which signifies for man the ultimate Either-Or, which constrains him to decision. The meaning of this decision becomes clearer when we consider further how Jesus' message of the Kingdom is related to the *Jewish eschatological hopes*. Obviously the Jews thought of the deliverance of the Kingdom of God as deliverance for the Jews. The Kingdom of God is at the same time the Jewish kingdom. (Daniel 2:44, 7:27) Even where the expectations have gone beyond the old national political boundaries, where God's world judgment of all men has replaced the downfall of nations overthrown for the benefit of Israel, where the material and nationalistic colors have been blended into the pictures of the heavenly glory, where the deliverance of the whole world is expected at the last day—even there the favored position of the Jewish people is taken for granted. The Messianic king of the last day is depicted after the model of the national Davidic dynasty; Jerusalem and its temple, though exalted to heavenly grandeur, are still in the final day of triumph symbols of Jewish glory. The hope of the return of the scattered lost tribes to the holy land is a constant element in the eschatological expectation. And obviously the overthrow of the Roman rule is equally necessary to the picture.

From Jesus we hear almost nothing of all these things. A clear impression of this difference can be derived from a comparison of the eschatological petitions of a Jewish prayer, the "Eighteen Benedictions," with the corresponding petitions of the prayer used in the circle of Jesus' disciples, the Lord's prayer. In the former the petitions run as follows:

"Look upon our need and guide our warfare
and redeem us for Thy name's sake.
Deliver us, O Lord our God, from the pain of our
    hearts,
and bring healing to our wounds.
Sound a great trumpet for our freedom
and raise the standard to bring back our exiles.
Bring back our judges as at the first,
and our counsellors as at the beginning.
Give no hope for the apostates,
and bring quickly to nought the kingdom of violence . . .
Have mercy, O Lord our God, on Jerusalem Thy city
and on Zion where Thy glory dwells,
and on the kingdom of the house of David,
the Messiah of Thy righteousness."

In the Lord's prayer we find only

> "Father, hallowed be Thy name,
> Thy Kingdom come,
> Thy will be done
> as in heaven, so on earth."

This is in agreement with the answer of Jesus to the question whether the Jews should pay tribute to Cæsar: "Give to Cæsar what belongs to Cæsar, and to God what belongs to God." (Mark 12:13–17) That is, the seeking after God is not to be confused with political desires. Similarly Jesus rejects the request to settle a quarrel over an inheritance: "Man, who made me a judge or arbiter over you?" (Luke 12:13, 14)

But unmistakable as the difference between the eschatological expectation of Jesus and the popular Jewish hopes is, it must neither be exaggerated nor, as is usually the case, misunderstood. The fact that in the thought of Jesus the national connotation of the Kingdom of God remains in the background does not mean that he taught its universality. He took for granted as did his contemporaries that *the Kingdom of God was to come for the benefit of the Jewish people.* Among his reported sayings are some in which the Kingdom of God is at the same time the kingdom of the faithful, who are comforted: "Fear not, little flock, for it is your Father's good pleasure to give you the Kingdom." (Luke 12:32, *cf.* Daniel 7:27) And a saying in a different form is preserved in which the chief authority in the Messianic age is promised to the Twelve as the representatives of the twelve tribes of the holy nation. (Matt. 19:28, Luke 22:29, 30) These are indeed not genuine words of Jesus; they reflect the hope of the earliest community, in which the Twelve were probably first chosen. But the history of this earliest community itself shows plainly that the preaching of Jesus had not extended beyond the boundaries of the Jewish people; he never thought of a mission to the Gentiles. The mission to the Gentiles came into being only after serious conflicts in the primitive church; and then the assumption was that such a mission was a way of adding to the chosen people, the *Jewish* Messianic community. The Gentile who wished to belong in the last day to the elect must be circumcised and keep the Jewish Law.

Out of such assumptions arose certain sayings which are put into the mouth of Jesus:

"Go not into any way of the Gentiles,
and enter not any city of the Samaritans,
But go rather to the strayed sheep of the house of
    Israel." (Matt. 10:5, 6)

And this natural limitation of the preaching to the Jews is naively expressed in the words:

"But when they persecute you in this city, flee into the next; truly I tell you, you shall not have gone through the cities of Israel till the Son of Man be come." (Matt. 10:33)

From the time of the controversy over the conversion of the Gentiles come the stories of the centurion in Capernaum and of the Syro-Phœnician woman. (Matt. 8:5–13 omitting verses 11, 12; Mark 7:24–30) These stories show that there are exceptions among the heathen who are worthy of being saved.

It is not impossible that the following saying goes back to Jesus himself.

"There shall be weeping and gnashing of teeth when you see Abraham, Isaac, and Jacob, and all the prophets in the Kingdom of God, and yourselves cast out. From east and west, from north and south shall men come, and shall sit down to eat in the Kingdom of God." (Luke 13:28, 29, *cf*. Matt. 8:11, 12)

Even if those who are to come from all directions to put to shame Jesus' fellow-countrymen are really Gentiles and not Jews of the dispersion, the words none the less naïvely assert that the chosen people and its heroes hold the central place in the Kingdom of God; afterward the Gentiles would join them, according to ancient prophecy. (*Cf*. Isaiah 2:1–3; 59:19) This is not an assertion that the Gentiles will come instead of the Jews, nor even that the Gentiles will come *like* the Jews; rather it is said that many Gentiles will come to shame the Jews. Further, the coming of the Gentiles does not mean that they join the actual historical community as a result of the preaching; it is rather a miraculous eschatological event. But the chief significance of this saying is negative: if many Gentiles are to bring the unrepentant Jews to shame, then clearly, belonging to the Jewish race does not constitute a right to a share in the Kingdom. Just this emphasis is characteristic of Jesus' conception, probably also of that of John the Baptist—the Jew as such has no claim before God. Consistently with this Jesus proclaims a call to decision and repentance. Consistently, too, Jesus can elsewhere picture a Samaritan as putting the true Jew to shame. (Luke 10:29–37)

3. *Universalism and Individualism? Dualism and Pessimism?*

This does not mean, however, that Jesus thinks in universalistic terms. Man as such has as little claim as the Jew. Jesus is far from seeing man in the light of humanism, as if by a natural endowment or by his destiny to realize an ideal, he possessed in himself divinity or kinship to God. *Thus the humanistic concept of universality is wholly foreign to him.* If the Kingdom of God were conceived universalistically, a claim of man upon God would be established. And it is exactly this claim which does not exist. It may indeed be said that there is a contradiction between the implication of the call to *repentance* addressed to the people, which does away with the claims of the nation as such, and the postulated limitation of the preaching to the Jews. This very contradiction shows clearly that man and the Kingdom of God are not seen by Jesus in the light of a humanistic ideal of mankind, that man as such is not predestined for the Kingdom. The Kingdom is an eschatological miracle, and those destined for it are not thus destined because of their humanity but because they are called of God. To begin with, the Jewish people are called, and the connection of the Kingdom with the Jewish people demonstrates most clearly how far from universalistic is the thought of the Kingdom, how utterly every human claim on God disappears; for the calling of the nation depends wholly on God's choosing. On the other hand, a nationalistic misinterpretation is avoided, since the call to repentance is directed to the chosen people, and this call rejects every claim of the individual based on the fact that he belongs to this people.

Thus *all humanistic individualism is rejected.* Not the individual but the "church" is called, to it belongs the promise. It is not the individual who attains, in the Kingdom of God, to the realization of his latent capacities, to the cultivation of his personality, or to perfect happiness. That *God* should cause His sovereignty to appear, that *His* will should be done, that the promise to the community should be fulfilled, this is what the realization of the Kingdom of God means. Thus the individual indeed finds deliverance, but only because he belongs to the eschatological community, not because of his personality. Further, the call to repentance guards against the misunderstanding that a man either could depend upon his calling or ought ever to despair of his calling. Through the call to repentance he is forced to decision, and his decision will show whether he belongs to the chosen or to the rejected.

Finally *all individualistic cultivation of the spirit, all mysticism, is excluded.* Jesus calls to *decision,* not to the *inner life.* He promises neither ecstasy nor spiritual peace; the Kingdom of God is not the object of occult vision and mystical raptures. The very naïveté of the heavenly banquet with Abraham, Isaac, and Jacob is significant. Jesus does not think of man in terms of the anthropological dualism of Hellenistic mysticism; that is, he does not speak of the tragedy of man, of the entangling of the divine soul in the earthly body, of its purification and liberation, either through cultic means or through contemplation, devotion, and absorption of self into the Infinite. The Kingdom of God is not a spiritual power or sphere, to which the highest in man is essentially akin, into which in certain spiritual experiences the soul enters. All pietistic religious experience is wholly alien to him. By any such means a claim of man on God would again be established, and man's attitude toward God would be that of raising himself to deity. Jesus knows only one attitude toward God—*obedience*. Since he sees man standing at the point of decision, the essential part of man is for him the will, the free act, and in this connection the dualistic anthropology which sees two natures, flesh and spirit, active in man, has no meaning. For on will, on free act, depends man's existence as a unit, as a whole; reflection on the antithesis of spirit and flesh has no place here. It is not the physical in man which is evil in him—the *whole* man is evil if his will is evil.

The Kingdom of God, then, is not to be understood in terms of a *metaphysical or cosmological dualism*. The present world is not deprived of value because of a *dualistic pessimism*. To what extent the well-known

48

sayings on the lilies of the field, the birds of heaven, and similar words were really spoken by Jesus can no longer be determined; they express the childlike faith in providence found in Jewish proverbial wisdom and that of the Orient in general. In any case the statement that in contrast to John the ascetic he was called a glutton and wine-drinker belongs to old tradition. (Matt. 11 :16–19) No word of complaint over the evil of the world, that it would be better never to have been born, that the beast is better off than man, such as the Jewish apocalypses contain, dominates the preaching of Jesus.

(One such saying is indeed inserted in the gospel record: "The foxes have holes and the birds of heaven their nests, but a son of man has nowhere to lay his head." (Matt. 8 :20) But this owes its inclusion among the words of Jesus to a misinterpretation. "A son of man" (human being) was understood as "the Son of man," and thus the saying was believed to embody a statement of Jesus about himself.)

To Jesus the world is not evil, but men are evil; and not in the sense that the human race as such is evil because of its lower nature. No, just as there are good and bad trees, so there are good and bad men; as the seed falls on good and bad ground, so the word of the gospel falls on good and bad hearts. There are healthy and sick, just and unjust. No theory of dualism, but the urgency of the demand leads to the insight that the will of men as a rule is bad, that before God at least none can be called good. (Matt. 7:11, Mark 10:8) But *the bad will is what makes the evil man evil,* the greedy hard-hearted, the religious self-complacent. The call to repentance includes all, and no one has any advantage over another or can look down on him. When he was told about the Galileans whom Pilate had slain, he said,

"Do you think that these Galileans were especially wicked, because this death came upon them? No, I tell you, but if you do not repent, you also will perish. Or do you think that those eighteen whom the Tower of Siloam fell on and slew were guiltier than the others in Jerusalem? No, I tell you; if you do not repent, you also will perish." (Luke 13:1–5)

The real evil in the world, then, is the evil will of men. Accordingly the "other world," the Kingdom of God, is not conceived as a universal metaphysical entity, as a finer, higher, more spiritual nature over against the earthly nature. The concept "Nature" has no place here. Except as the God-given world in which man receives the gift of God and must prove himself obedient to God's will, "nature" for Jesus does not exist. Thus the question of how far the present earthly nature is to be changed or replaced through the coming of the Kingdom is not relevant. Just as the present world exists only as God's creation, so the world to come also will be His creation. Therefore the Kingdom of God cannot be for Jesus a colorful realm of fancy to which the individual can flee for refreshment and escape from responsibility.

4. *Future and Present. The Necessity of Decision*

The future Kingdom of God, then, is not something which is to come in the course of time, so that to advance its coming one can do something in particular, perhaps through penitential prayers and good works, which become superfluous in the moment of its coming. Rather, the Kingdom of God is a power *which, although it is entirely future, wholly determines the present*. It determines the present because it now compels man to decision; he is determined thereby either in this direction or in that, as chosen or as rejected, in his entire present existence. Future and present are not related in the sense that the Kingdom begins as a historical fact in the present and achieves its fulfillment in the future; nor in the sense that an inner, spiritual possession of personal attributes or qualities of soul constitutes a present hold on the Kingdom, to which only the future consummation is lacking. Rather the Kingdom of God is genuinely future, because it is not a 'metaphysical entity or condition, but the future action of God, which can be in no sense something given in the present. None the less this future determines man in his present, and exactly for that reason is true future—not merely something to come "somewhere, sometime," but destined for man and constraining him to decision.

The coming of the Kingdom of God is therefore not really an event in the course of time, which is due to occur sometime and toward which man can either take a definite attitude or hold himself neutral. Before he takes any attitude he is already constrained to make his choice, and therefore he must understand that just this necessity of decision constitutes the essential part of his human nature. Because Jesus sees man thus in a crisis of decision before God, it is understandable that in his thought the Jewish Messianic hope becomes the absolute certainty that in this hour the Kingdom of God is coming. If men are standing in the crisis of decision, and if precisely this crisis is the essential characteristic of their humanity, then every hour is the last hour, and we can understand that for Jesus the whole contemporary mythology is pressed into the service of this conception of human existence. Thus he understood and proclaimed his hour as the last hour.

This message of the Kingdom of God is absolutely alien to the present-day conception of humanity. We are accustomed to regard a man as an individual of the species "man," a being endowed with definite capacities, the development of which brings the human ideal in him to realization—of course with variations in each individual. As "character" or as "personality," man achieves his end. Harmonious development of all human faculties, according to the individual endowment of each man, is the way to this ideal. Perhaps no man can travel this road to the end, but progress along the road, bringing the ideal nearer to realization, justifies human existence. We are accustomed to distinguish between the physical or sensuous and the mental or spiritual life. And even if at the same time the connection between them is assumed, and symmetrical development is the shining goal, still the spirit is the guiding principle, and the life of the spirit is the true meaning of human existence.

All this is completely alien to the teaching of Jesus. Jesus expresses no conception of a human ideal, no thought of a development of human capacities, no idea of something valuable in man as such, no conception of the spirit in the modern sense. Of the spirit in our sense and of its life or experience, Jesus does not speak at all. The word which in the English Biblical translations is generally rendered "soul" or "spirit" usually means simply "life," as in the well-known saying: "What shall it profit a man if he gains the whole world and loses his soul?" (Mark 8:36) The meaning is simply: Of what use are all the possessions of the world to a man who must die? The greed of man for property and profit is here shown to be as absurd as in the story of the rich farmer.

"There was a rich man whose land had yielded well. And he thought to himself, What shall I do? I have no place to put my grain. And he said, This is what I will do; I will pull down my barns and build greater ones, and there I will put all my grain. And then I will say to my soul [*i.e.,* simply "to myself"], Soul, you have much wealth stored up for many years; rest, eat,

53

drink, and be merry. But God said to him, Fool, to-night your soul [*i.e.*, your life] will be taken, and who then will own your possessions?" (Luke 12:16–20)

The modern conception differs fundamentally from that of Jesus, because the former assumes the *intrinsic worth of humanity,* at least of the highest and noblest in it. The highest in man, indeed, is often designated without qualification as divine. By way of contrast, the worth of a man for Jesus is not determined by his human quality or the character of his spiritual life, but simply by the decision the man makes in the here-and-now of his present life. Jesus sees man as standing here and now under the necessity of decision, with the possibility of decision through his own free act. Only what a man now does gives him his value. And this crisis of decision arises for the man because he is face to face with the coming of the Kingdom of God. Somewhat similarly one might see the essential quality of human life defined by the fact that death awaits men and by the way they allow themselves to be determined thereby. And indeed the Kingdom of God and death are alike in this—that both the Kingdom and death imply the end of earthly human existence as we know it, with its possibilities and interests. Moreover it may be said that death, like the Kingdom, is not to be considered by man as an accidental event, which sometime will bring to an end the everyday course of life, but as the true future which confronts man and limits him in the present and puts him under the necessity of decision. Thus in either case the judgment is pronounced upon man not from the human standpoint, as if man's value were somehow immanent and securely possessed by him, but from without—according to Jesus, of course, God is the only Judge.

However, the coming of the Kingdom of God differs from the coming of death, because death is darkness, silence, while the Kingdom is a positive promise to man. Evidently when a man is constrained by the inevitable coming of death to make the decision, this decision can have only a negative sense, that is, to live his present life as a dying man, as an alien. On the contrary the decision which is forced upon him because of the coming of the Kingdom is positive—that is, to act in his present life in accordance with the will of God. What positive meaning "to do the will of God" has for men has yet to be determined from the teaching of Jesus.

First, it must again be stressed that the eschatological message of Jesus, the preaching of the coming of the Kingdom and of the call to repentance, can be understood only when one considers the *conception of man which in the last analysis underlies it,* and when one remembers that it can have meaning only for him who is ready to question the habitual human self-interpretation and to measure it by this opposed interpretation of human existence. Then it becomes obvious that the attention is not to be turned to the contemporary mythology in terms of which the real meaning in Jesus' teaching finds its outward expression. This mythology ends by abandoning the fundamental insight which gave it birth, the conception of man as forced to decision through a future act of God. To this mythology belongs the expectation of the end of the world as occurring in time, the expectation which in the contemporary situation of Jesus is the natural expression of his conviction that even in the present man stands in the crisis of decision, that the present is for him the last hour. To this mythology belongs also the figure of Satan who now fights against the hosts of the Lord. If it is true that to Jesus the world can be called bad only in so far as men are bad, that is, are of evil will, then it is clear how little the figure of Satan really meant to him.

Finally, it is also clear why Jesus cannot give a description of the Kingdom of God. Any such description would be possible only by projecting the demands and ideals of man or his spiritual experiences into the other world; and thereby the essential character of the beyond would be taken away. The Kingdom would be a creation of human desire and imagination; it would not be the Kingdom of *God*. But the Kingdom of God is not something dark, silent, and unknown, so that the idea of its relation to man is based wholly on speculation; rather the will of God is a comprehensible concept for men. What does it mean?

III

The Teaching of Jesus: The Will of God

1. Jesus as Rabbi

We begin at this point because we are seeking to move inward from the periphery to the centre—that is, we begin with the attempt to understand the ethical teaching of Jesus as it appears within the framework of the thought of his contemporaries.

Whoever would characterize Jesus on the basis of his eschatological message alone would call him "prophet," the title given to the Baptist. (Mark 11:32; Matt. 11:9) Actually Jesus himself is several times called prophet, even though his followers, who believed him to be the Messiah, considered that too limited a title for him. (Mark 8:28; Matt. 21:11, 46; Luke 7:16, 39; 13:33; 24:19; *cf.* Matt, 12:39) But besides "prophet" another designation of Jesus appears in the gospels: he is addressed as "rabbi." (Mark 9:5; 10:51; 11:21; 14:45)

This title, which in the Greek gospels is usually rendered by the ordinary Greek form of address (Lord, Sir), marks Jesus as belonging to the class of scribes. And that implies, if it is to be taken seriously, that Jesus, being a scribe, had received the necessary scribal training and had passed the requisite scribal tests. Although we are uncertain how strictly the course of study which is known from the rabbinic literature was regulated at the time of Jesus, and although we probably should assume that it was less defined than a century later, yet we must not ignore Jesus' title of Rabbi. He was called, so to speak, "Professor," "learned Doctor," and that surprises us, since we have from his eschatological message gained the impression of him as a prophet. Is it perhaps true that this prophet came forth from the ranks of the scribes? That the preaching of the Baptist first uprooted him from the circle of the devotees of the Law, that then he became the prophet who spoke with authority and not as the scribes? Of all that we know nothing.

But if the gospel record is worthy of credence, it is at least clear that *Jesus actually lived as a Jewish rabbi.* As such he takes his place as a teacher in the synagogue. As such he gathers around him a circle of pupils. As such he disputes over questions of the Law with pupils and opponents or with people seeking knowledge who turn to him as the celebrated rabbi. He disputes along the same lines as Jewish rabbis, uses the same methods of argument, the same turns of speech; like them he coins proverbs and teaches in parables. Jesus' teaching shows in content also a close relationship with that of the rabbis. The question, "Which is the chief commandment?" (Mark 12:28–34) was often discussed by them, and was even answered in the same way—love to God and one's neighbor.

Sayings like these come down to us from the rabbis:

"Have you ever seen an animal or a bird ply a trade? And yet they are fed without anxiety. And they are created to serve me; but I was created to serve my Creator. Therefore I ought to be able to feed myself without anxiety." (*Cf.* Matt. 6:26)

"Do not worry over tomorrow's cares, for you do not know what the day will bring. Perhaps you will not be alive tomorrow, and then you would have tortured yourself over matters which no longer concern you. There is enough trouble for each hour." (*Cf.* Matt. 6:34)

"A man is measured by the measure with which he measures." (*Cf.* Matt. 7:2)

"If he knocks, it will be opened for him." (*Cf.* Matt. 7:7)

"If the bird is not caught without the will of heaven, how much less we." (*Cf.* Matt. 10:29)

"A man does not hurt his finger unless it was willed in heaven." (*Cf.* Matt. 10:30)

"Be not like servants who serve their master because of the need of wages. Be rather like servants who serve their master without need of wages." (*Cf.* Luke 17:7–10)

"He who is richer in learning than in good actions, to what should he be compared? To a tree whose branches are many but whose roots are few. If a wind comes, it uproots it and fells it. But that man whose actions are greater than his learning, to what should he be compared? To a tree whose branches are few but whose roots are many. If all the winds in the world storm against it, yet they cannot move it from its place." (*Cf.* Matt. 7:24–27)

"A man who does good deeds and who learns much of the Law, to whom is he like? To a man who builds a foundation of stone, and above it mud brick. Then when much water beats upon it, yet it does not wash it from its place.

"And a man who does no good deeds and who learns the Law, to whom is he like? To a man who builds first with mud bricks and then sets stone upon them. If even a little water comes, it carries them away." (*Cf.* Matt. 7:24–27)

"Take a man who loses a Sel'a or some other coin in his house. He lights many lamps and candles, till he finds it. Judge now from small to great. If a man lights many lamps for the sake of those things which preserve only the life of an hour in this world, do you not need to seek earnestly for the word of the Law which preserves life both in this world and in the world to come?" (*Cf.* Luke 15:8, 9)

This list could be easily continued; and indeed such examples must be kept in mind in order to understand how Jesus taught as a Jewish rabbi.

As it is important that he is addressed as Rabbi, so also it is significant that his adherents (not the twelve only) are called pupils (disciples). That too is a technical term, and designates the pupils of a rabbi, not the members of a religious fellowship. In the Christian community this title as the designation of Christians was soon replaced by others (brothers, saints). Paul no longer called the Christians disciples, since he could no longer conceive of Jesus as a rabbi. Only under the influence of the gospels was the term "pupil" used for a while in the later literature, crystallizing the ecclesiastical use of "disciple," restricting it to the twelve, as is usual today.

It may be, as was said above, that at the time of Jesus the practices of the scribal profession were less fixed than two generations later, and it may also be true that Jesus was less bound by forms than other rabbis. One may at this point note that among his adherents were women, who are elsewhere never included among the followers of a rabbi. His intercourse with sinners, prostitutes, and publicans, which is surely historical, is also alien to the practices of a rabbi. If the tradition in this respect is reliable, he showed especial affection for children, a trait which does not correspond to the typical figure of a rabbi. All this makes the picture of his ministry more complex, one might say richer; but because of the fragmentary nature of the sources we can no longer see the whole clearly. However we cannot doubt that the characteristics of a rabbi appeared plainly in Jesus' ministry and way of teaching, unless the tradition has radically distorted the picture.

2. *The Authority of Scripture*

Jesus agreed always with the scribes of his time in accepting without question the *authority of the (Old Testament) Law*. When he was asked by the rich man, "What must I do to inherit eternal life?" he answered, "You know the commandments," and he repeated from the well-known Old Testament decalogue, "Do not kill, nor commit adultery, nor steal, nor accuse falsely, nor covet; honor your father and your mother." (Mark 10:17–19) To the man who asked him about the chief commandment, he cited two passages of the Old Testament Law (Deut. 6:4, 5, Lev. 19:18): "The first is this: Hear, O Israel, the Lord our God is God alone. Love the Lord your God with all your heart and with all your soul and with all your mind and with all your strength. The second is this: Love your neighbor as yourself." (Mark 12:28–31) When he was asked about divorce, he again appealed to two passages of the Law (Gen. 1:27 and 2:24): "Man and woman He created them; therefore a man will leave father and mother, and the two become one flesh." (Mark 10:6–8) Similarly in other cases. (*Cf.* Mark 2:25–26; 12:26; Matt. 9:13; 12:7)

Certainly there is no guarantee that all the sayings in the gospels in which Jesus cites words of Scripture were really spoken by him; many were surely put into his mouth by the church, in order to justify its own position. But the very attitude of the church is significant; it could not possibly have taken for granted the loyal adherence to the Law and defended it against Paul, if Jesus had combated the authority of the Law. Jesus did not attack the Law, but assumed its authority and interpreted it. That this interpretation often did violence to the original meaning of the Law, that Jesus' own course of action on occasion was opposed to the Law, is a different matter, and is not inconsistent with his belief that he found in the Law the will of God. It was sometime after his death, when Paul and other Hellenistic missionaries preached to the Gentiles a gospel apart from the Law, that the attitude toward the Law was recognized as a problem in the community. Only then did they reflect upon the question of the Law's validity. And from this time come the well-known words, which Jesus surely cannot have said: "Do not suppose that I have come to destroy the Law and the Prophets, I have not come to destroy but to fulfil. I tell you truly, until heaven and earth vanish, no letter nor point can vanish from the Law until all is fulfilled. Whoever erases one of the smallest commandments and so teaches others shall be called least in the Kingdom of Heaven. But whoever keeps it and teaches it will be called great in the Kingdom of Heaven." (Matt. 5:17–19)

This much is evident, that the idea that Jesus had attacked the authority of the Law was wholly unknown to the Christian community. Jesus did this as little as he opposed worship in the temple. The continuance of the temple worship and the sharing in the offering of sacrifice is presupposed in the sayings of Matt. 5:23–24, and it is clear from the legend of the coin in the fish's mouth (Matt. 17:24–27) that the community still paid the temple tax. Also Jesus did not oppose the religious practices which were customary for pious Jews, almsgiving, prayer, and fasting. He protested only against observing them for the sake of personal vanity, and insisted that they be done silently with a sincere heart. (Matt. 6:1–4, 5–8, 16–18) Even the saying, "Can the wedding guests fast when the bridegroom is still with them?" (Mark 2:19) involves no fundamental rejection of fasting, but implies that in the joyful Messianic age now beginning fasting has lost its meaning. But this asserts rather than denies that for mourners fasting is natural. The similes of the new patch on the old garment and of new wine in the old wineskins (Mark 2:21–22) are susceptible of several interpretations (for example, in the joy of the Messianic age the ancient mourning customs no longer have meaning); but the original significance of the words can no longer be ascertained.

Jesus asserted the authority of the Law; his characteristic attitude to it can be found only by asking how he understood it. For *the essential fact about a teacher is not his acceptance of an authoritative mass of tradition, but the way in which he interprets it.* And at this point the difference between Jesus and the Jewish legalistic piety becomes clear. Both the rabbis and Jesus explained the Law; and at this point both agreement and difference are shown.

3. The Jewish Ethic of Obedience

For Jewish legalistic religion as well as for Jesus, the
statement holds that not adherence to the Law but understanding of the Law is the characteristic element.
For Jewish religion as for Jesus the multifarious laws
of the Old Testament had in great part lost their original meaning. This is clear from the fact that the
Old Testament Scripture—laws, historical books and
prophecies—were for Judaism a unity, that the distinction between different stages of Old Testament religion
and morality was not felt at all.

In the Old Testament the stages of national and
cultic religion and their regulations are found con-
fusedly mingled. The standpoint of *national religion*
appears in the utterances in which God's interests are
identified with those of the people, when for example
Israel's war is assumed to be God's war, Israel's honor
God's honor, Israel's country God's country. It is
shown also in the social laws, which were to keep the
life of the people healthy and vigorous. The standpoint
of *cultic religion* appears not only in the legislation for
temple and sacrifice, but also in all the ritual regulations
which burdened the life of the individual. The primitive
conceptions of clean and unclean lie at the bottom of
these rules; there are certain things and certain events
in natural human life (like birth and death) which
bring man under the influence of mysterious dæmonic

forces; there are actions and situations in life which are full of these dangerous powers or are threatened by them. For all such cases complicated rules are necessary in order to avoid the dangers connected with them. Thence arise the regulations about sacrifices, cleanness and uncleanness, marriage, dead bodies, and the rest.

In later Judaism the laws of the national code had largely lost their original meaning under the pressure of the wholly changed political conditions and partly changed economic conditions. God was no longer the God of the holy land, but the Lord of the world. The regulations for cult and ritual were no longer understood in their original sense. But all the old regulations were preserved; they were sanctified by the authority of Scripture, and they were to be scrupulously observed because they were commanded by God. Obligation to obedience depended no longer upon content but upon formal authority; not *what* was commanded determined the will of the person acting, but the fact *that* such and such was commanded. This attitude could endure, because along with these national and cultic laws the Old Testament contains also an abundance of universal ethical precepts for the permanent relationships between man and man, for situations of life which remain essentially the same in all ages. Thus the verdict of the moral consciousness expressed itself in precepts such as are formulated in the decalogue, or in the preaching of the prophets with their demand for justice and righteousness, instructions of universal validity which were obeyed not only because of the formal authority but because they command a morality consistent with conscience.

It cannot be said however that the religion of later Judaism was determined by the prophetic preaching. For its peculiar characteristic is the conviction that because of the formal authority of Scripture all the commands of the Law are equally binding. Also Palestinian Judaism did not avail itself of an allegorical interpretation of the mass of incomprehensible and impracticable commands in order to find in them an intelligible moral meaning. This method was used only in Hellenistic Judaism under the influence of Greek thinking, as it was later in the Christian church, when it needed to come to terms with the Old Testament laws. Rather, *the commandments were kept because they were commanded.* Perhaps here and there the idea entered in, that through such laws as those of circumcision and the Sabbath the chosen people was separated from the Gentiles and designated as belonging to God. But that is not the main point; the fundamental desire is to be obedient to the sacred Law, without reference to what it commands. *Obedience* is the essence of Jewish morality. This is well expressed in the words of a rabbi, who declines to discuss any critical question on the content of the law of purification, explaining that the content is irrelevant: "Death does not make unclean, nor water clean. But the Holy One has said, I have established a Law, have fixed a decree; you are not to transgress my decree, which is written; this is the distinguishing mark of my Law."

As an *ethic of obedience* the Jewish morality was not designed from the human standpoint; that is, its purpose is not the realization of an ideal of man or of humanity. It is definitely opposed to all humanistic ethics, for in it not man but only the glory of God is important. A basis for what is good and is therefore required of man cannot then be established by reference to some conception of man, by derivation from the rational ideas which are inherent in the mind of man. Hence the idea of moral personality is lacking, and there is no real doctrine of virtue, like that which developed in connection with the Greek conception of man, and which Philo was soon to make acceptable to Alexandrian Jews under the influence of Greek philosophy. The true Jew does not know the concept "virtue" at all, and has no word for it. Hence the notion of an ideal of human society, which is to be realized through human activity, is wanting; there can be no analogy here to the Greek idea of the State. Obviously there can be no so-called value-ethic here either, where nothing has value in itself. Only obedience gives an action its significance.

Since this obedience is obedience to a *purely formal authority,* in the late Jewish ethic there appears the commingling of moral and ritual laws, and the over-emphasis on ritual and ceremonial rules, which Jesus denounces in the statement that the Pharisees strain out gnats and swallow camels. (Matt. 23:24) This is also the reason for the preponderance of prohibitions (there are 365 as compared with 278 positive commands), and for the infinitely detailed requirements, for the lack of broad moral principles, and for the total ignoring of important aspects of life. The ideal religious Jew is accordingly the man who studies the Law of the Lord day and night, who knows how to find, through ingenious interpretations of the Law, the necessary rules of conduct for each situation of life and every relationship. Just because conduct is not determined by unified intelligible basic principles, but is regulated by the formal authority of the Law, the task of the scribe is to "make a fence around the Torah," that is, by endless acute deductions from Scripture to find rules for cases not foreseen in the Law, which nevertheless confront men in their present life.

It is indeed true that a way out of this multiplicity and diversity was striven for; the scribes at the time of Jesus discussed the question of the central requirement of the Law, and they sought to classify, to combine, or to set up certain moral principles as fundamentally important. "Love your neighbor as yourself" one rabbi cited as the quintessence of the Law. Another, "What you do not wish done to you, do to no one else." A third, "It is all one, whether a man does much or little, if only he turns his heart toward heaven (that is, toward God)." Simplicity and singleness of heart, that a man should completely will the good, is designated in a Jewish writing (the Testaments of the Twelve Patriarchs) as the true requirement of God. And there developed the formulation of universal ethical precepts which were valid also for the Gentiles, the "Way on earth."

Criticism of formal legalism also exists. From the rabbis a statement comes down to us similar to that which according to Christian tradition Jesus uttered, "The Sabbath is given to you, not you to the Sabbath." (*Cf.* Mark 2:27) Among the rabbis too the principle is accepted that one may break the Sabbath in order to save a life. But when we read with what casuistic rules the practical following of this principle is burdened, we see that the fundamental idea of the Jewish ethic, blind obedience, still dominates. The will of God is the formal authority of Scripture; ethic is therefore not distinguishable from law.

Along with this view, belief in the *meritoriousness* of conduct according to the Law easily established itself. In fact the dependence on good works, the pride in good works, evidently played a fatal part in late Judaism. The religious man expects to be able to call God's attention to his merits, he believes that he has a claim on God. This comes to expression especially in the idea that over and above performance of duty there are some acts beyond duty—good works, such as alms-giving, prayer, and fasting. The relation to God is thus conceived as a legal contract relation; God must reward the righteous and punish the wicked. An index of this conception is the absurd dispute in which several rabbis engaged: what will become of the men whose good and bad deeds are equal?

At the same time we should utterly misunderstand the Jewish ethic if we supposed that it was entirely dominated by thought of reward. However popular this idea may have been among the lower classes, it does not give Jewish religion its peculiar character. Rather the fundamental trait of this religion is *obedience*. Obedi-ence which is not the fulfillment of a contract, but which arises from reverence before the majesty of the holy God. That the conduct of man should not proceed from selfish aspiration after benefits, but from the fear of God, "in the name of" God, is again and again em-phasized as a protest against the morality motivated by desire of reward. "If you have kept the Law, count it not merit, since for that you were created," runs a rab-binical maxim. And the word of Rabbi Antigonus of Socho (of pre-Christian times) has already been cited: "Be not like servants who serve their master because of the need of wages. Be rather like servants who serve their master without need of wages."

One should not, then, designate the Jewish ethic as an ethic of works and contrast it with an ethic of intention. For since finally only one thing, obedience, is required, the Jewish ethic is throughout an ethic of *motive*. It is not *completely* so, since in Jewish thought motive has no intrinsic value, is not viewed as an attribute of man or as an inherent tendency of the human will. Obedience is not to be considered in this sense, as an attribute—it is far more closely related to activity, thus it is not a quality of the ideal man (in which case man would again be regarded humanistically), but is actual only in the instant of action. Moreover obedience is possible only because man stands immediately under the authority of God. The motive of obedience is, then, something which a man dependent on himself, as the Greek conceived him, cannot possess, for he recognizes no authority to which there could be any question of obedience; he knows only the law of the perfecting of his own nature by his own achievement.

4. *Jesus' Insistence on Obedience*

The fundamental tendency and consequences of this Jewish ethic of obedience must be kept in mind by any one who desires to understand *Jesus' preaching of the will of God* and who would comprehend its agreement with Jewish religion as well as its divergence. He will then also understand its difference from the Greek ideal of man and from the modern rationalistic ethic of autonomy or the recent ethic of value. This can be put in a sentence—the ethic of Jesus, exactly like the Jewish, is an ethic of obedience, and the single though fundamental difference is that Jesus has conceived radically the idea of obedience. But what this means must now be considered, and illustrated by the words of Jesus.

Jesus sees the conduct of man from the view-point of the obedience which man owes to God. Two parables show this plainly:

"Which of you says to his ploughman or herdsman, when he comes home from the field, Come here and sit down at the table? Does he not say instead, Get my dinner ready, put on an apron, and wait on me; afterward you can eat and drink! He will surely not thank the servant because he did what was ordered. So you must say, when you have done all that was ordered, We are servants, we have done only our proper work." (Luke 17:7–10)

"The Kingdom of Heaven is like a farmer who went out early in the morning to hire workmen for his vineyard. When he had agreed to pay them a silver piece a day, he sent them into his vineyard.

"And at the third hour he went out and saw others standing idle in the market place and said to them, Go also into the vineyard, and I will give you what is right. And they went.

"Again he went out at the sixth hour and at the ninth, and did the same. Finally he went out at the eleventh hour, and found others standing there, and said to them, Why do you stand here all day doing nothing? They said, No one has hired us. He said, You too go into the vineyard.

"In the evening the owner of the vineyard said to his overseer, Call the workmen and pay them, beginning with the latest comers. Then came those of the eleventh hour, and each received a silver piece. When the first came, they thought they would receive more; but they also each received a silver piece. Then they grumbled against the farmer and said, These last have worked only an hour, and you have paid them the same as us who have worked the whole day and borne the heat. But he answered, My friend, I do you no wrong; did you not agree to work for a silver piece? Take what belongs to you and go. I choose to give these last as much as I give you. Can I not do what I want with my own money? Are you envious because I am generous?" (Matt. 20:1–15)

Both parables express as strongly as possible the conviction that man can have no claim on God. And to this extent Jesus is completely in agreement with those rabbis who present the fundamental ideas of the Jewish ethic. But the obligation to a purely formal authority which must be blindly obeyed receives from Jesus a transformation which goes beyond anything known to us in contemporary rabbinic criticism.

This divergence is shown in his use of Old Testament Scripture. Its authority is absolute for him as for the rabbis. And that which distinguishes him is not merely the sureness with which, in questions as to the way of life or the chief commandment, he chooses from the Law the ethical commands as alone binding; (Mark 10:19, 12:29–31) for even on this point Jewish teachers stand beside him. But in contrast to the scribal assumption that all passages of Scripture are equally binding and that apparent contradictions are to be reconciled, Jesus sets one passage against another. Though it is written in the Law of Moses that the husband can divorce his wife with a bill of divorcement, on the other hand it is written, "God created them man and woman; therefore a man shall leave father and mother, and the two shall be one flesh. What God has joined, man must not separate." That, and not Moses' law of divorce, is God's will; Moses wrote this only "because of your hard-heartedness." (Mark 10:2–9) Clearly then it is not the formal authority which is binding on men; if a man can make such distinctions in Scripture, evidently the insight to recognize what is demanded by God is attributed to him. It is also clear that the content of the command is not a matter of indifference, but it is the content itself which determines whether a word of Scripture is God's command or not. This view, which distinguishes critically between the essential and the non-essential in Scripture, is expressed in the saying:

"Woe to you, scribes and Pharisees! You tithe mint, anise, and cummin, and ignore the most important part of the law—justice, mercy, and truth. These men must do and not leave out the other. You blind guides, who strain out a moth and swallow a camel!" (Matt. 23:23, 24)

Although the form of these words is conservative (do this, and do not leave that out), yet the formal, external authority of Scripture is evidently given up. This becomes fully clear from a series of *controversial sayings* and *scenes of conflict;* these received their detailed formulation from the early church, but here the attitude of the church is the best witness for the teaching of Jesus. The practices of external cleansing are called hypocrisy, with a quotation from the prophet Isaiah: "This people honors me with their lips, but their heart is far from me. They worship me in vain, with their teaching of the precepts of men." (Mark 7:6-7) The scribes have nullified the word of God; for it is commanded, "Honor your father and your mother: and whoever reviles father and mother shall be put to death." Now if any one by oath withdraws the property which he owes to his parents from secular use and declares it holy, the scribes hold this oath to be more sacred than the duty of a son. (Mark 7:9-13)

In such polemic Jesus apparently intends to attack merely a particular scribal interpretation of the Old Testament. Actually he opposes not only a whole group of Old Testament laws, but the Old Testament itself as formal legal authority. The whole law of purification is nullified by the saying, "There is nothing which comes into a man from without which defiles him; it is what comes out of a man which defiles him." (Mark 7:15)

What God's will is, is not stated by an external authority, so that the content of the command is a matter of indifference, but man is trusted and expected to see for himself what God commands. God's requirements are intrinsically intelligible. And here the idea of obedience is first radically conceived. For so long as obedience is only subjection to an authority which man does not understand, it is no true obedience; something in man still remains outside and does not submit, is not bound by the command of God. Criticism can still arise: *in itself* this does not concern me, *in itself* these things are indifferent—but *I choose* to obey. In *this* kind of decision a man stands outside of his action, he is not *completely* obedient. Radical obedience exists only when a man inwardly assents to what is required of him, when the thing commanded is seen as intrinsically God's command; when the whole man stands behind what he does; or better, when the whole man is *in* what he does, when he is not *doing something obediently,* but *is* essentially obedient.

There is also one more point of difference. With the attitude that obedience is subjection to a formal authority to which the self can be subordinated without being essentially obedient, a neutral position is possible. Man is so to speak only accidentally or occasionally claimed by God, and it is possible to suppose that he might not be so claimed, that this demand of God probably sometimes ceases because it is not an essential element of the human self before God. Indeed this position is not only possible but actual, for instance when a man finds himself in a situation to which no rule in the Scripture, the formal authority, applies. Hence according to the rabbinical view, man is in the happy position of being able to do more than is expected, to do works of supererogation, that is, to do something pleasing to God where nothing in particular is commanded by God. Hence too there are situations in which it is possible for a man to do nothing—neutral situations. And just this Jesus expressly denies. To the accusation that he was breaking the Sabbath to help a man, he answered, "Ought a man to do good or evil on the Sabbath? save a life, or kill?" The implication is that there is no third way besides doing good or doing evil; to do nothing in this case would be equivalent to doing evil. There is therefore no neutral position; obedience is radically conceived and involves man's whole being. This means that the whole man is under the necessity of decision; there is no neutrality for him, he has to decide between the only two possibilities which there are for his life, between good and evil.

But it may be asked, is not this demand of radical obedience contradicted by the thought of *reward,* which Jesus uses quite simply as the basis for the requirement, as threat or promise? He promises for example a reward in heaven; (Matt. 6:19, 20; Mark 10:21, and elsewhere) he threatens with the fire of hell. (Matt. 10:28; Mark 9:43-47, and elsewhere)

The thought of reward stands in a peculiarly para-doxical, perhaps contradictory, relation to the demand for obedience. But it is absolutely clear that Jesus demanded obedience without any secondary motive. The parables of the servant who had no claim to the thanks of his master and of the workmen in the vineyard (Luke 17:7–10, Matt. 20:1–15) distinctly oppose all human calculation of rewards from God, expressly deny that man can have any sort of claim before God. But Jesus is wholly certain that man *does* receive re-ward or punishment from God. And the words in which Jesus speaks of these possibilities are meant to call men's attention to the consequences of their conduct. These consequences cannot serve as the motive in the exact sense, where the idea of obedience is completely carried through. How would the command to love, for example, be possible? For love with the secondary motive of reward, love with a backward look on one's own achievement, would not be love. Jesus' attitude is indeed paradoxical; he promises reward to those who are obedient without thought of reward.

But the idea of reward he holds firmly. Here too he recognizes only an Either-Or; either reward from man or reward from God, but reward awaits every right action. (Matt. 6:1–4, 5–8, 16–18) In this respect Jesus again differentiates his thought sharply from the *idealistic ethic.* He knows nothing of *doing good for good's sake;* the idea that every good deed is its own reward is foreign to him. For with this idea the humanistic conception of man is again presupposed, the conviction of the intrinsic worth of the human. According to Jesus' view man does not win value for himself, but if he is obedient God rewards him, gives him more than he has. This can be made clear from the fact that in the relation between man and man the actual reward for kindness shown is not the kindness itself, but the joy and gratitude which are awakened by it and enrich the giver. This reward can evidently never become the motive of the act, and nevertheless we should misunderstand and fail to appreciate what happens between man and man, if we did not see that for the kindness of man this reward is promised. So also the man who is obedient is enriched by God. At this point Jesus' conception is opposed to a specifically ascetic attitude, that is, to the belief that self-annihilation is the behavior demanded of men by God. Self-denial and sacrifice are indeed required of man; but God is not represented as a selfish tyrant whose requirement means death for man. His demand means life; behind the demand stands the promise.

From the requirement of radical obedience Jesus gains the right to brand as incomplete and hypocritical the conventional piety, which gives itself airs and prides itself on its correctness. For where the thought of obedience is not taken completely in earnest and a man sees his obedience always as his own achievement, there the spirit of self-righteousness and pride enters in. And even if the religious man makes no claim on God, still he looks down on those who cannot show the same correctness of external obedience. So Jesus rebukes the people who give their alms in the synagogues and on the streets, who stand and pray on the street corners, who when they fast show mournful faces in order that their piety may be seen (Matt. 6:2, 5, 16)—the people who exhibit themselves as good before men; God however sees the heart, and what is honored by men is an abomination before God. (Luke 16:15)

"Woe to you, scribes and Pharisees, hypocrites!
You clean the outside, cup and platter,
But within you are full of theft and greed.
Woe to you, scribes and Pharisees!
You are like whitewashed graves, which look neat
    outside,
but within are full of dead bones and filth.
So you appear righteous before the people,
but within you are full of hypocrisy and wickedness."
                                    (Matt. 23:25, 27, 28)

In these words there is expressed the scorn of men who reckon their fidelity to the Law as a noteworthy achievement, who in spite of all submission to the Law are yet not inwardly obedient. The words are therefore, quite apart from the question of how far they actually apply to the character of scribal religion, an assertion of the demand for complete obedience.

And in truth just this demand for complete obedience

which involves the whole man takes a heavy burden from man, however paradoxical this sounds; for he is now set free from the endless and useless task of searching for commands and prohibitions which he must know in order to act rightly; from the fear of having failed here and there because he did not know the scriptural precept or its right interpretation; from the contempt which was felt for the people who did not know the Law. As long as the Old Testament is the formal authority, and scribal explanation and exegesis must mediate its meaning for all practical situations of life, only the scribe can really be obedient, and whoever belongs to the "people who do not know the Law" is inevitably obliged to be a sinner.

From Rabbi Hillel this saying is preserved: "There is no uneducated man [that is, no one not a scribe] who fears sin. Not one of the 'people of the land' [that is, no one who belongs to the common people] is religious." Jesus denounces the scribes who pile heavy burdens on men, which they themselves will not raise a finger to lift. (Matt. 23:4)

"Woe to you, scribes and Pharisees, hypocrites!
You close the Kingdom of Heaven to the people.
You yourselves do not enter, and you do not let in
    those who wish to enter." (Matt. 23:13)

Jesus knows that he is called to sinners as the physician to the sick. (Mark 2:17) He clearly implies that they have a better understanding of the will of God than the impeccable. Perhaps this is the point of the saying, "I praise Thee, Father, Lord of heaven and earth, that Thou hast hidden this from the wise and clever and hast revealed it to the simple. Yes, Father, so hast Thou decreed" (Matt. 11:25, 26) His opponents reproached him with being a friend of tax collectors and sinners. (Matt. 11:19, *cf*. Mark 2:16) His church received the impression of him which it expressed by putting into his mouth these words (probably originally from some wisdom book, describing the God-given Wisdom):

"Come to me, all you weary and burdened,
I will give you rest.
Take my yoke upon you and learn from me,
For I am kindly and gracious,
So you will find rest for yourselves;
For my yoke is easy,
and my burden is light." (Matt. 11:28–30)

The obedience for which Jesus asks is easy, because it frees a man from dependence on a formal authority, and therefore frees him also from the judgment of the men whose profession it is to explain this authority. Such obedience is easy, because it depends on the judgment and responsibility of the one concerned. Of course from another angle it is all the more difficult. For to the weak man it is a relief to have the judgment of good and evil and all *responsibility* taken away from him. And *this* burden is just what Jesus puts upon men; he teaches men to see themselves as called to *decision*—decision between good and evil, decision for God's will or for their own will.

The liberation which Jesus brings does not consist in teaching man to recognize the good as the law of his own human nature, in preaching autonomy in the modern sense. *The good is the will of God, not the self-realization of humanity, not man's endowment.* The divergence of Jesus from Judaism is in thinking out the idea of obedience radically to the end, not in setting it aside. His ethic also is strictly opposed to every humanistic ethic and value ethic; it is an ethic of obedience. He sees the meaning of human action not in the development toward an ideal of man which is founded on the human spirit; nor in the realization of an ideal human society through human action. He has no so-called individual or social ethics; the concept of an ideal or end is foreign to him. The concepts of personality and its virtues and of humanity are also foreign to him; he sees only the individual man standing before the will of God. Conduct moreover is not significant because a value is achieved or realized through action; the action as such is obedience or disobedience; thus Jesus has no system of values.

This really means that *Jesus teaches no ethics at all* in the sense of an intelligible theory valid for all men concerning what should be done and left undone. Such a theory, whether it be idealistic or utilitarian, can proceed only from a well-defined view of man as a being with particular capacities and particular ends. Such a theory makes man—even though it be the ideal man—the measure of human action; and it looks upon man as essentially secure, controlling all the possibilities of action. Jesus sees man and his life very differently—as absolutely insecure before what confronts him. A man cannot control beforehand the possibilities upon which he must act; he cannot in the moment of decision fall back upon principles, upon a general ethical theory which can relieve him of responsibility for the decision; rather, every moment of decision is essentially new. For man does not meet the crisis of decision armed with a definite standard; he stands on no firm base, but rather alone in empty space. This it is which shows the requirement of the good to be actually the demand of God—not the demand of something divine in man, but the demand of God who is beyond man.

This view also parts company with the *idea of development,* according to which the moral judgment of man develops or the man himself develops and perfects himself. Here there is no relative standard, only the absolute. The decision is an absolute Either-Or; the good which is here required is not a relative good, which on a higher level of development can be replaced by something better—it is the will of God. And man in this situation does not decide whether he will climb higher or sink lower, but whether he is righteous or a sinner. To be a sinner does not mean to stand on a relatively low level of morality, but means to be rejected of God. It is thus clear that Jesus has no such concept as "morality." The concepts "morality" and "moral development," however much meaning and justification they may have in other connections, are excluded for Jesus, because he sees man in the crisis of decision, and because for him the concepts "good" and "bad" depend upon the will of God.

Hence it is misleading to set Jesus' moral teaching as an "ethic of intention" over against the Jewish "ethic of works." For the former phrase fits the moral teaching of Jesus as little as the latter is a correct characterization of the Jewish ethic. So far as the obedience demanded *is* intention, "intention" applies equally to the ethic of the rabbis and to that of Jesus. The more radical conception of obedience held by Jesus involves of course a clearer conception of this intention. Meanwhile, the significance of obedience is not that it is a habit of man's inner life, an attribute of man which gives him as such a moral quality. With Jesus as in Judaism, obedience is bound up with the crisis of decision in which man stands; obedience is actual only in the moment of action, and if one wishes to call obedience an intention, he must at the same time hold fast the fact that this obedience presupposes the authority of God. Man can be obedient only in answer to this authority; as soon as man is considered as existing for himself alone, he cannot be obedient.

5. *The Intelligibility of the Demand*

What is the intrinsic significance of the demands of God? They are not mediated to man through Scripture as a formal authority (for then they would not be intrinsically intelligible), and they are not derived from an ideal picture of man and humanity. They cannot be deduced from a universal ethical theory. Then whence do they come? They arise quite simply from the crisis of decision in which man stands before God. This answer has meaning, of course, only for him who sees man, who sees himself, forced to this necessity of decision. Its meaning is simply that this moment of decision contains all that is necessary for the decision, since in it the whole of life is at stake. The man, who enters the present moment with his past still clinging to him, is put in a critical position precisely as the man which through his past he has become; staking all, he stands before the future. It is not for him a matter of choosing this or that from the variegated bundle of future possibilities, according to the standards brought with him out of his past; these very standards are in question. The man does not in reality choose something for its own sake, but with every choice he decides and limits his own possibility.

In this crisis of decision, the continuity with the past is accordingly abrogated and the present cannot be understood from the point of view of development—

though in other connections, when man is thought of as an observer, continuity may have a valid meaning. The crisis of decision is the situation in which all observation is excluded, for which *Now* alone has meaning, which is absorbed wholly in the present moment. *Now* must man know what to do and leave undone, and no standard whatsoever from the past or from the universal is available. *That* is the meaning of decision.

This of course does not mean that man lacks insight into the practical possibilities of his conduct and its consequences, which is drawn from empirical precedents. Decision is not dice-throwing; its character becomes plainer the more clearly the empirical possibilities are understood. Decision means that the choice between the possibilities is not determined by the insight into them but is free and responsible. Whoever sees man in the crisis of decision and recognizes this as the essential of human existence, assumes that man knows what is *now* good and evil; as has already been said, he knows, not on the basis of any past experience or rational deductions, but directly from the immediate situation.

Hence there is naturally no longer reason to formulate general ideas about the highest good, about virtues and values, for every such theory originates from the spectator's point of view. In the view of Jesus there can be no such ethic, and therefore it is fundamentally a mistake to look to him for concrete ethical requirements or for his attitude toward concrete ethical problems. He always refers the questioner back to his own judgment. It is almost superfluous to add that there are no really new ethical precepts of Jesus, that his specific sayings have numerous parallels in the Jewish tradition.

The only possible method, then, is to gain from the words of Jesus some conception of what he understood by obedience to the will of God. The demands of the Sermon on the Mount have always been regarded as particularly characteristic of the preaching of Jesus. Here we find at the beginning the new set over against the old in strong antitheses, in a peculiar interpretation of the Old Testament which evidently aims to establish its true meaning as against the scribal interpretation, thus completely destroying, as we have before observed, the formal authority of Scripture. In this connection it is of no significance that probably only three of the following six passages originally had the impressive antithetical form, while the other three were compiled after their model from other sayings of Jesus.

"You have heard that it was said to men of old, Do not kill; whoever kills shall incur judgment. But I tell you, Every one who is angry with his brother shall incur judgment." (The following is probably later elaboration: "and who says to his brother 'fool' shall incur heavy penalty, and who says 'idiot' shall incur hell fire.") (Matt. 5:21, 22)

"You have heard that it was said, Do not commit adultery. But I tell you, Every man who looks at a woman to desire her has already committed adultery with her in his heart." (Matt. 6:27, 28)

"Further it was said, He who sends away his wife must give her a writ of divorce. But I tell you, He who sends away his wife and marries another commits adultery, and he who marries a divorced woman commits adultery." (Matt. 5:31–32 or Luke 16:18)

"Also you have heard that it was said to men of old, Do not swear falsely, but keep your oath to the Lord. But I tell you, do not swear at all; your word must be yes for yes, no for no; whatever goes beyond that is evil." (Matt. 5:33, 37)

"You have heard that it was said, Eye for eye, and tooth for tooth. But I tell you, Do not defend yourselves against injury; whoever strikes you on the right cheek, offer him the other; whoever goes to law with you about your cloak, give him your coat also; whoever forces you for a mile, go two with him." (Matt. 5:38–41)

"You have heard that it was said, Love your neighbor and hate your enemy. I tell you, Love your enemies and pray for your persecutors, that you may be sons of your Father in heaven. For He lets His sun rise on the evil and on the good, and lets it rain on the just and the unjust. For if you love only those who love you, what have you done? Do not the tax-collectors do that? And if you greet your brothers only, what especial thing do you do? Do not the Gentiles also do that? You must be perfect, as your heavenly Father also is perfect." (Matt. 5:43–48)

In all these passages the decisive requirement is the same: the good which is to be done is to be done *com-*

pletely. He who does it partially, with reservations, just enough to fulfill the outward regulation, has not done it at all. He who indeed refrains from murder but does not master anger has not understood that he must decide completely. He who indeed avoids adultery, but keeps lust in his heart, has not understood the prohibition of adultery, which requires of him complete purity. He who refrains simply from perjury has not seen that absolute truthfulness is demanded. He who divorces his wife has not understood that marriage requires of him a complete decision, but thinks of it as a relative action which can be annulled. He who takes revenge for injustice does not realize that by so doing he himself upholds injustice; to reject injustice completely means not to retaliate. He who is kind only to friends does not know what love means; for complete love includes love of enemies. The meaning of this statement may be thus interpreted: Jesus sets the demand of law over against the demand of God. The Old Testament commands to which Jesus opposes "But I say unto you" have for the Jews a purely formal authority, the character of law. Law claims a man so far as his conduct can be bound by formulated precepts. Beyond these it leaves free play to man's self-will. Jesus' belief is on the contrary that the human will has no freedom before God, but is radically claimed by Him. Under the law, the question "How well does my conduct conform to the commandment?" becomes a question of content, of the

What of the action. Obedience to the law must be determinable, and therefore law must concern itself with the
What of action, not the *How*. Hence formal obedience
to the law as such is no radical obedience, though of
course true obedience can exist in fulfillment of the law.

Jesus has wholly separated obedience from legalism;
hence he does not set up a better law in opposition to a
less good law; he opposes the view that the fulfillment
of the law is the fulfilling of the will of God. For God
demands the whole man, not merely specific acts from
the man.

Jesus then sees the act as expressing the *whole* man,
that is, he sees his action from the view-point of decision: Either-Or. Every half-way is an abomination. It
would obviously be a complete misunderstanding to
take these "But I tell you" passages as formal legal
precepts of an external authority, which can be fulfilled
by outward behavior. Whoever appealing to a word of
Jesus refuses to dissolve an unendurable marriage, or
whoever offers the other cheek to one who strikes him,
because Jesus said so, would not understand Jesus. For
he would have missed exactly the obedience which
Jesus desires; he would imagine that he could achieve
and present an act of obedience when obedience is not
really present as the determining factor of his life. All
these sayings are meant to make clear by extreme examples that it is not a question of satisfying an outward
authority but of being *completely* obedient. It is also

wholly impossible to regard Jesus' teachings as universally valid ethical precepts by which a man can once for all order his life. Unless the decision which is demanded in these sayings arises out of a present situation, it is not truly the decision of obedience, but an achievement which the man accomplishes; he stands outside his action, is not wholly identified with it.

Are not the demands of Jesus, then, impossible for man as we know him? For we cannot escape by saying, it depends only on the intention—thus separating the intention from the deed and seeing behind the deed an ideal of conduct which perhaps will be realized sometime in the future, if only the good intention is kept alive in the man and he is more and more educated to that end. Jesus does not reckon with such a future; the future which Jesus knows is not that of man but of God, not under the control of man but predestined for man. He does not see the intention as something supratemporal in man, so that a man's mistake in the present can be compensated for from some later standpoint. Rather he sees the concrete man in the crisis of decision, and the decision is not relative but absolute. A man's failure or mistake in the present has in the eyes of Jesus not the relative character of a stage of development, but the absolute character of sin; for Jesus sees man as before God.

The requirements of the Sermon on the Mount do not present an ethical idealism, but bring to light the absolute character of the demands of God. How little they may be understood in the sense of ethical idealism is clear from the fact that the command of love explains nothing concerning the content of love. *What* must a man do to love his neighbor or his enemy? It is said simply *that* he is to do it. What a man ought *not* to do is stated; but does not the command of love thus remain colorless and devoid of content? It is clear that an ethic which is based upon the ideal of man or humanity could present concrete requirements of *how* love must be practised, *what* one must do—at least under particular conditions—in order to make man or humanity happy. Jesus knows nothing of such concrete demands, and cannot know them, since he asks what is good from the standpoint not of man but of God; he can only leave the decision to the man in his concrete situation. If a man really loves, he knows already what he has to do.

This finds expression in the parable of the talents.

"For it is as if a man decided to travel, and called his servants and entrusted his property to them. To one he gave five talents, to the second two, to the third one, each in proportion to his ability, and then he departed. Then the one who had received five talents put them to use and earned with them five talents more. In the same way he who had been given the two gained two more. But he who had received one, went off, dug a hole, and buried his master's talent.

"After a long time the master of those servants came and asked for their accounts. Then came he who had received the five talents and brought the other five talents and said, Master, you gave me five talents, here are five more which I have earned. His master said to him, O good and faithful servant, you were faithful in little, I will put you in charge of much; come and join in the joy of your master.

"Then came also he who had received the two talents and said, Master, you gave me two talents, here are two more which I earned. His master said to him, O good and faithful servant, you were faithful in little, I will put you in charge of much; come and join in the joy of your master.

"Then came also he who had received the one talent and said, Master, I know that you are a hard man, that you reap where you have not sown and gather where you have not scattered; and in fear I went out and hid your talent in the ground. But his master answered him, Lazy and wicked servant, did you know that I reap where I have not sown and gather where I did not scatter? Then you should have taken my money to the bankers, and at my return I should have received my money back with interest. Therefore take the talent from him and give it to him who has ten. For to him who has shall be given, so that he has abundance; and from him who has not, even that which he has will be taken. And cast the worthless servant out into the dark; there will be wailing and gnashing of teeth." (Matt. 25:14–30)

The responsibility is put on man; he must answer for his own actions; they are regarded as the expression of his being, and by them he is judged. This is the meaning of the words:

"Can men gather grapes from thorns,
or figs from thistles?

Every tree is known by its fruit.
A good tree cannot bear bad fruit."
                    (Matt. 7:16, 18 or Luke 6:43, 44)

"The eye is the light of the body.
If your eye is clear,
Your whole body will be in the light;
But if your eye is good for nothing,
Your whole body will be in darkness."
                                (Matt. 6:22, 23)

Such a man, who in contrast to those learned in the Law really understands what is demanded of him in the given situation, is depicted in the story of the good Samaritan. Luke reports it, pertinently for content if somewhat awkwardly from the point of view of style, as told by Jesus in answer to the evasive question "Who is my neighbor?"

"A man was going down from Jerusalem to Jericho and fell into the hands of thieves. They stripped him, wounded him, and left him lying half dead. By chance a priest came that same way, saw him, and went by. Also a Levite came to the place, saw him, and went by. But a Samaritan who came along the road found him, looked at him, and pitied him. He went to him, bound up his wounds, and poured oil and wine on them. Then he put him on his beast, brought him to an inn, and cared for him. The next morning he took out two coins, gave them to the inn-keeper, and said, Look after him; what more it costs you, I will pay when I come back. Which of these three was neighbor to him who fell among thieves?" (Luke 10:30–36)

Other sayings of Jesus are intended to bring to men's

consciousness the *absolute character of the divine demand,* and to show that a man cannot follow the will of God together with his own interests; it is a question of Either-Or.

"As he went along the road, a man came running to him, knelt before him, and asked, Good master, what must I do to inherit eternal life? But Jesus said to him, Why do you call me good? No one is good but God alone. You know the commandments: do not commit adultery, do not kill, do not steal, do not accuse falsely, do not covet, honor father and mother. He said, All that I have done from childhood. Jesus looked at him, loved him, and said, You lack one thing; go, sell all that you have, give it to the poor, then you will have a treasure in heaven; and come and follow me. He was grieved at this and went sadly away; for he was very rich." (Mark 10:17–22)

Two things the story shows: first, that man cannot maintain the cause of God merely up to a certain point, so far as may be without disturbing himself; rather the will of God claims the man completely. Mark has emphasized this further, by adding to the story some other words of Jesus, "How hard it is to enter the Kingdom of God! It is easier for a camel to go through the eye of a needle than for a rich man to enter the Kingdom of God." The other point is this—that Jesus makes the rich man realize that his formal goodness does not help him. Truly when a man asks after the way of life, there is nothing in particular to say to him. He is to do what is right, what every one knows. But if then a speciai demand confronts the man, it becomes plain whether the *whole* man was involved in that right conduct, whether that doing of what is right really rests on the decision for the good. Otherwise it has no worth. Expressed in Oriental fashion, it depends on where the heart is, with God or with the world.

"Do not collect for yourselves treasures on earth,
where moth and rust destroy them,
and where thieves break in and steal.
But gather for yourselves treasures in heaven,
where moth and rust do not destroy,
and where no thieves break in and steal.
For where your treasure is, there is your heart also."
(Matt. 6:19–21)

Perhaps it is an old Oriental proverb that Jesus or the church has appropriated and used to make clear to the hearer the Either-Or:

"No one can serve two masters.
Either he must hate one and love the other,
or he must hold to one and despise the other.
You cannot serve God and Mammon." (Matt. 6:24)

6. *Ascetism and World Reformation*

The words in which Jesus attacks wealth must not be misunderstood as meaning that he made the general demand that every one should give away his property, that he preached the ideal of poverty or demanded asceticism. The conception of an ideal which is to be realized through action is, as we have seen, foreign to

Jesus. Not a *state* to which man can attain through his conduct is considered good, but the *deed* alone is good or bad. Jesus simply sees how wealth claims its possessor, makes him a slave, and robs him of the freedom to decide for God. His words indeed say plainly that whoever follows Jesus must have the strength and freedom to renounce his possessions. But it is equally plain that he does not mean to say that by voluntary poverty a man wins for himself a special quality in the sight of God; not *poverty* but *surrender* is demanded. The conduct of the early Christian community makes this quite clear; for in it poverty was by no means felt as an advantage but as real distress. Of course the wealthy members of the church gave up their property for the common good, but voluntarily as an offering, not in order to gain especial saintliness. Nowhere in early Christian preaching is the ideal of poverty taught; it was only later that such ideas gained influence on Christianity. The early Christians, following Jesus, used the childlike prayer, "Our daily bread give us today."

Jesus desires no asceticism, he requires only the strength for sacrifice. As little as he repudiates property as such does he reject marriage or demand sexual asceticism. The ideal of virginity indeed entered Christianity early; we find it already in the churches of Paul. But it is entirely foreign to Jesus; he required only purity and the sanctity of marriage. Of course he required renunciation of marriage also as a sacrifice under certain circumstances. (Matt. 19:12) But there is no word from him which declares the sexual life, the physical as such, to be evil, or which ascribes to the state of virginity an especial sanctity. Here too the conduct of his church is clear proof; many of his disciples, Peter included, were married, and no one thought of demanding renunciation of marriage.

Moreover fasting as an ascetic exercise was not required by Jesus. He recognized it as an allowable religious practice if it comes from the heart. (Matt. 6:16–18) But fasting as an act pleasing to God, through which a man attains to an especially holy state, he did not know. He was reproached as a glutton and drinker, in contrast to John the Baptist, who was an ascetic. (Matt. 11:19) In the church the custom of regular fasts on two week days was soon adopted in imitation of the Jewish custom; but even in the church the custom was not a sign of asceticism, not a means to holiness.

Jesus, then, in no sense desires asceticism, and this is highly characteristic of his whole attitude and shows how he regards the position of man before God. The demand for asceticism really rests on the assumption that man through his behavior can attain a certain ideal or saintly quality which remains with him as a possession. The emphasis shifts accordingly from the behavior, the action, to that which is achieved thereby.

Action loses its absolute character as the moment of decision, when subordinated to the view-point of the end, the ideal. This ideal may be the Greek ideal of the harmonious, independent man, complete in himself like a work of art; then asceticism becomes a technique of spiritual discipline, of character development, somewhat as in the Stoic philosophy. This may be called the *asceticism of self-improvement*. Or the ideal may be determined by the assumptions of religious dualism, that the material world, the body, the senses, are evil, and that man must raise himself out of this lower nature to the divine nature. Since Deity neither eats nor drinks, neither sleep nor begets, man must as far as possible renounce all these things in order to attain divine holiness. In a heightened emotional, life, in visions and ecstasies, as they are induced or furthered by such abstinence, the ascetic believes he already finds traces of this divine nature in himself. This kind of asceticism may be called the *asceticism of sanctification*.

Jesus is far removed from both kinds of asceticism. They have in common the goal of the abundant life for men. But this is not for Jesus the essential meaning of human life; for him its meaning is that man stands under the necessity of decision before God, is confronted by the demand of the will of God, which must be comprehended in each concrete moment and obeyed. Man does not have to achieve for himself particular qualities, either an especial virtue or an especial saintliness; he must simply be obedient, and for that he needs no special qualities. God is not far from him, so that a technique is necessary to approach Him; on the contrary, God speaks to him in every concrete situation, for every concrete situation is a crisis of decision. Man has, so to speak, no time for any preoccupation with asceticism.

In the concrete situation, that is, in this world, in this nature, man stands before God; there is no need of escaping beyond the present or outside of nature. Nowhere does Jesus say that nature is evil, that therefore one ought not to have this or ought not to do that. The will of the man who is disobedient is evil; it is for him to surrender, not to deny nature. Jesus, as we have already seen, does not have the concept "nature" at all. Since he sees the life of man as determined by God, besides God no other powers exist with which man must deal in order to reach God. Rather, that which we call nature comes into consideration only so far as it characterizes that present condition of men which is determined by the necessity of decision. That is, nature as "objective," which can be observed separately from the action of men, does not come in question, except as it presents the manifold possibilities for human conduct.

Hence not even God Himself can be considered under the category of nature. And all asceticism of sanctification, which aims to attain for itself the divine nature, must be wholly foreign to Jesus. For him there is no such thing as a *divine nature;* that is a specifically Greek idea. God is for Jesus the Power who constrains man to decision, who confronts him in the demand for good, who determines his future. God therefore cannot be regarded "objectively" as a nature complete in itself, but only in the actual comprehension of his own existence can man find God. If he does not find Him here, he will not find Him as a "nature."

The consequences of this idea of God can be carried still further. Here it is important first to recognize that for Jesus the will of God in no sense means the demand for asceticism, that his attitude toward wealth as toward all "natural" gifts is determined by the idea of surrender. Therefore Jesus' *attitude toward property* cannot be explained from social ideals or from any socialistic and proletarian instincts and motives. It is true that the poor and hungry are blessed, because the Kingdom of God will end their need (Luke 6:20, 21), but the Kingdom is no ideal social order. Subversive ideas and revolutionary utterances are lacking in Jesus' preaching. There were splendid buildings erected under Herod and his successors in Jerusalem and other Jewish cities—palaces, theatres, hippodromes—but no mention of them occurs in the gospel record; from the gospels we learn nothing at all about the economic situation in Palestine, except that there were peasants and fishermen, hand workers and merchants, rich and poor

—and all this only incidentally, mostly from the parables. Then we see clearly that all these things played no rôle in the thought of Jesus and his community, that they did not look with envious and longing eyes toward worldly splendor. Jesus' imagination did not concern itself with pictures of the overthrow of wealth or with hopes of achieving still greater splendors.

There is only one passage in the gospel record in which a rich man is declared deserving of hell-fire simply because he is rich, and a poor man simply because he is poor is found worthy to be carried by the angels to Abraham's bosom—the story of the rich man and Lazarus. (Luke 16:19–26) This is unique, and is probably not a genuine part of the preaching of Jesus.

Jesus does not ascetically renounce this world and its institutions, nor measure it critically by the standard of a social ideal, neither does he give positive worth to the duties which grow out of life in this world. *No program for world-reformation is derived from the will of God.* He does not speak of the value of *marriage* and the *family* for personality and for society. He speaks indeed of the holiness and indissolubility of marriage for him who has contracted it. (Matt. 5:31, 32; Luke 16: 18) But he demands also the dissolving of all family relationships and the renouncing of marriage as a sacrifice which may be required as an act of decision (Matt. 8:22, 19:12; Luke 14:26)—as he himself sends away his relatives and calls those who do the will of God his brothers and sisters. (Mark 3:31–35) His attitude is therefore characteristically two-sided and will be misunderstood by any one who has not grasped the idea of decision. Neither marriage nor celibacy is in itself good; either can be demanded of a man. How each individual must decide, he will know, if he seeks not his own interests but the will of God.

Jesus speaks of *property* only as he does of *wealth,* that it becomes a fetter to man; that property can be used otherwise than for one's own enjoyment, that is, for service to the common good, as when it serves as a means of production—this idea is completely outside the thought of Jesus, and can well remain so. For every one has to decide for himself whether his own property is of this character; and no economic theory about the productive value of property relieves him from the responsibility of his own decision.

Of the value of work Jesus does not speak. Here it is again made plain that he is not interested in character building, personality values, and the like. Just as little does Jesus think of the value of work for society and civilization. Just as we cannot deduce that for man as Jesus sees him, before God, work can never be a duty (for this is left to the decision of the individual), so also it is clear that in the view of Jesus there can be no thought of the universal value of work. It is an alternative for which decision may be required, but not a demand valid for all.

Jesus, unlike the Old Testament prophets, does not speak of the state and civil rights. The polemic of the prophets against worship of false gods in Israel was combined with the struggle against political and social wrongs. Their preaching demanded justice and right- eousness for the common people, and their demand was asserted by them as a command of God. The words of Jesus in the Sermon on the Mount show that Jesus sets the requirement of law and justice over against the com- mand of God.

Nevertheless there is a fundamental likeness between the prophetic conception of the will of God and that of Jesus. The prophets were combating a type of religion which assumed that men could satisfy the will of God through careful observance of the cult and ceremonial cleanliness, and could in other matters follow their own will. In opposition to such a view and to the levity, cruelty, and social injustice which grew out of it, the prophets proclaimed justice and right as the demand of God. The significance of law and justice to them was that it set bounds to man's self-will and controlled the community life by its requirements. But history showed—here as elsewhere—that man understands how to bend the law which he should serve to his own service. He understands how to combine obedience to the letter of the law with the attainment of his own desires; he knows how to stand on his own rights precisely in rela- tion to the neighbor to whose service the law should compel him.

Because he realized this corruption of man, Jesus did not endeavor (as we have already seen) to create a better law, but he showed that the will of God, which *can* manifest itself *in* the law, claims man beyond the requirement of the law. This naturally does not mean that Jesus wished to abrogate law for human society, that he—as Tolstoi misunderstood him—advocated anarchy. It means simply that Jesus saw his task not as the founding of an ideal human society, but as the proclaiming of the will of God. Undoubtedly his expectation of the imminent coming of the Kingdom of God excluded the question of practical regulations for nation and state from the centre of his thought. This explanation however does not suffice, because if Jesus had taken any interest at all in the construction of a social order, his predictions of the Kingdom would have shown traces of this interest, as the Jewish Messianic hope did. A Jewish Messianic psalm, for example, runs thus:

"He will gather a holy people and rule them in righteousness,
He will give justice to the tribes of the nation sanctified by the Lord their God,
And He will let injustice endure no more in the midst of them,
And no one may dwell with them who has dealing with evil,
And He will distribute them by their tribes over the land,
And no foreigner or stranger can live with them any more.

He will speak justice to nations and tribes in the wisdom of His righteousness." (Ps. Sol. 17:28–31)

The hope of Jesus never includes these elements, and from this it must be fully understood that his only purpose is to make known the position of man before God. What possibilities of political action may arise for the individual from this position, what in the concrete case his concrete duty is, he must himself decide. Although there is one saying attributed to Jesus which promises the position of authority in the Kingdom to the "twelve" (Matt. 19:28 or Luke 22:29), on the whole even in the early Christian community political desires and fancies have seldom found a place in connection with the hope for the Kingdom of God.

The will of God is then for Jesus as little a social or political program as it is either an ethical system which proceeds from an ideal of man and humanity or an ethic of value. He knows neither the conception of personality nor that of virtue; the latter word he does not even use, it is found first in Hellenistic Christianity. As he has no doctrine of virtue, so also he has none of duty or of the good. It is sufficient for a man to know that God has placed him under the necessity of decision in every concrete situation in life, in the here and now. And this means that he himself must know what is required of him, and that no authority and no theory can take from him this responsibility.

If a man is really capable of meeting this responsibility, he is like the good tree which bears good fruit; then his "heart" is good; and "the good man brings good out of the good treasure of his heart, and the evil man out of the evil brings evil." (Luke 6:45) Whoever sees a wounded man lying on the road knows without further command that it is right to help him. Whoever encounters the sick and oppressed knows that no Sabbath ordinance can hinder the duty to help. In all good conduct it is revealed whether the man desires to do God's will, that is, whether he wills to be completely obedient, entirely renounce his own claims, surrender his natural will with its demands. This in itself implies the requirement of truth and purity, and the casting aside of all hypocrisy, vanity, greed, and impurity. Such a man needs no particular rules for his conduct toward other men; his conduct is determined by renunciation of his own claim.

"You know that the princes of the nations
are those who lord it over them,
and their great men rule them by force;
but it is not to be so among you;
rather he who will be great among you,
let him be your servant,
and he who will be the first among you,
let him be the servant of all." (Mark 10:42–44)

"You are not to let yourself be called Rabbi,
for one is your teacher, that is, God; but you are all
    brothers.
And do not call anyone father on earth,

for one is your Father, who is in heaven.
The greatest among you shall be your servant.
He who exalts himself shall be humbled,
and he who humbles himself shall be exalted."

(Matt. 23:8–9, 11–12)

7. *The Commandment of Love*

The requirement for conduct toward others may then be epitomized in the commandment of love. This commandment is generally accepted as the essentially Christian requirement, as the new ethic which Jesus taught. But if Jesus' requirement of love is to be correctly understood, two points must first be considered. First, that the word "love" and the command to love appear relatively seldom in the words of Jesus; indeed only in the Sermon on the Mount as the requirement of love for enemies (Matt. 5:43–48) and in the answer to the question about the chief commandment as the requirement of love of neighbor which stands next to the love of God. These are emphatic passages, but they are so few that it is plainly to be seen that neither Jesus nor his church thought of establishing by this demand for love a particular program of ethics. Rather the demand for love is included under the general requirement of doing the will of God; or better expressed, the will of God, in so far as it determines conduct toward other men, may be designated as the commandment of love.

This definition brings us to the second point, that neither Jesus nor his church thought that the command to love was a new requirement which had been hitherto unknown. In fact not only does "Love your neighbor as yourself" serve in Jewish literature as a summary of the Law (Paul too says in Rom. 13:8–10 that love means the fulfillment of the Law), but also in pagan literature love—love of man and even love of enemies —is regarded as one of the highest virtues. It appears for example in the writings of the Stoic philosopher Seneca: "Let us not grow weary of laboring for the general welfare, of helping individuals, of giving aid even to enemies." In another passage he protests against the objection of natural feeling: "But anger is refreshing—it is a satisfaction to requite injury!" He answers: "No! It is indeed worthy of honor to requite good with good; but not injustice with injustice. In the former it is ignominious to be conquered; here it is ignominious to conquer."

But it is evident that here the requirement of love is based upon the idea of humanity. It belongs to the ideal of man that he should not let himself be moved out of his repose, out of the harmony of his spiritual equilibrium, by any injury which overtakes him. That would be ignominious. He must have such control over himself, be possessed of such moral energy, that he is elevated above anger and the desire of revenge. If some one strikes him, that disturbs him no more than if an ass had kicked him; if he is spit upon, it affects him no more than if the sea had sprinkled him with its foam. Who would get excited over that? The basis of Jesus' demand for love is entirely different—not the conception of strength of character and personal worth, but the concept of obedience, of renunciation of one's own claim.

One more difference must be noted. In the classical literature the requirement of love is based on still another idea, which Seneca clearly expresses in the brief words: "Man is for man something holy." This motivation too is derived from man; the intrinsic value of man is assumed as something certain, objective. Because man is valuable, worthful, holy, the demand for love of man, philanthropy, is valid; and its highest consummation is love for enemies. Jesus does not support his demand for love by referring to the value of other men as human beings, and love of enemies is not the high point of universal love of humanity, but the high point of overcoming of self, the surrender of one's own claim.

Jesus thought of love neither as a virtue which belongs to the perfection of man, nor as an aid to the well-being of society, but as an overcoming of self-will in the concrete situation of life in which a man encounters other men. Hence Jesus' requirement of love cannot be more nearly defined in content, or be regarded as an ethical principle from which particular concrete requirements can be derived, as would be possible with the humanistic command of love, which depends on a well-defined ideal of humanity. *What* a man must do in order to love his neighbor or his enemy is not stated. It is assumed that every one can know that, and therefore Jesus' demand for love is no revelation of a new principle of ethics nor of a new conception of the dignity of man. In love man does not gain infinite spiritual value and thereby obtain a share in the divine essence; love is simply the requirement of obedience and shows how this obedience can and ought to be practised in the concrete situation in which man is bound to man.

This follows from the conjunction of the command of love for neighbor with the command of love for God. This connection is not in itself a new idea which Judaism had never before known. This can be seen from the narrative in which the question of the chief commandment occurs.

"A scribe came, who had heard them [Jesus and the Sadducees] arguing, and noticed that Jesus had answered them well. He asked him, What command is the first of all?

"Jesus answered, The first is this: Hear, O Israel, the Lord our God is Lord alone, and you shall love the Lord your God with all your heart and with all your soul and with all your strength. The second is this: Love your neighbor as yourself. There is no commandment greater than these.

"Then the scribe said to him, Master, you have spoken truly; there is One, and none beside Him. And to love Him with all the heart and with all the understanding and with all the strength, and to love one's neighbor as oneself, is worth more than all burnt-offerings and other sacrifices.

"And Jesus saw that he had answered intelligently, and said to him, You are not far from the Kingdom of God." (Mark 12:28–34)

It can and must be said that this double command wins its full significance only when it appears in connection with the preaching of Jesus. Its meaning then is this: the two commands, to love God and to love one's neighbor are not identical, so that love of neighbor would be without anything further love for God. This misunderstanding can arise only when neighbor-love is taken in the philanthropic sense, when an intrinsic worth, something divine, is ascribed to man. Then truly the relation to God has been lost and for it a relation to men has been substituted. You cannot love God; very well, then, love men, for in them you love God. No; on the contrary the chief command is this: love God, bow your own will in obedience to God's. And this first command defines the meaning of the second—the attitude which I take toward my neighbor is determined by the attitude which I take before God; as obedient to God, setting aside my selfish will, renouncing my own claims, I stand before my neighbor, prepared for sacrifice for my neighbor as for God.

And conversely the second command determines the meaning of the first: in loving my neighbor I prove my obedience to God. There is no obedience to God in a vacuum so to speak, no obedience separate from the concrete situation in which I stand as a man among men, no obedience which is directed immediately toward God. Whatever of kindness, pity, mercy, I show my neighbor is not something which I do for God, but something which I really do for my neighbor; the neighbor is not a sort of tool by means of which I practise the love of God, and love of neighbor cannot be practised with a look aside toward God. Rather, as I can love my neighbor only when I surrender my will completely to God's will, so I can love God only while I will what He wills, while I really love my neighbor.

This love, although not a principle from which concrete requirements can be derived, is by no means so without content that I must ask, What am I then to do, in order to love? Whoever so asks has plainly not understood the words "Love your neighbor as yourself." For what it means to love *himself,* he knows very well, and without any theory or system about the self. For self-love is not a principle of morality, but the attitude of the natural man. If a man then is to love his neighbor as himself, he knows very well how to direct his conduct in the concrete situation. Kierkegaard was right when he said, "If a man is to love his neighbor *as himself,* the command turns the lock of the stronghold of self-love as with a master key and casts self-love out. Were the command of neighbor-love expressed otherwise than by the little phrase 'as yourself,' which is so easy to grasp and yet has the reach of eternity, the command could not so master self-love. This 'as yourself' cannot be twisted nor subtly rationalized. With the penetrating keenness of the eternal it presses into the farthest corner in which a man loves himself; it leaves self-love not the slightest excuse, nor the smallest loophole. How wonderful! One could give long and ingenious discourses on how a man should love his neighbor, and self-love would still always know how to bring forward excuses and evasions, because the subject is not covered, one case would be overlooked, one point would be not exactly or strictly enough expressed and described. But this 'as yourself'—no wrestler can grip his opponent so closely, with a hold so inescapable, as this command grips self-love."

It is therefore stupid to say—and this again is possible only in association with the humanistic ideal of man—that a justifiable self-love, a necessary standard of self-respect, must precede love of neighbor, since the command runs "love your neighbor *as yourself.*" Self-love is thus presupposed. Yes, it is indeed presupposed, but not as something which man needs to learn, which must be expressly required of him. It is the attitude of the natural man which must be overcome.

One requirement among others of this love of neighbor is the readiness to *forgive* one's neighbor, and this readiness characterizes most distinctly the love which is here demanded. For if the thought of forgiveness is taken seriously, this requirement is the most difficult which natural self-love encounters. To renounce revenge, to do good to the enemy, even to pray for him—to all this a man can force himself. But to forgive him? This is possible only if one really loves him. But how seriously the demand for forgiveness is intended, Jesus shows in his answer to the question, "How often must I forgive my brother when he sins against me? Are seven times enough?" Jesus answers, "I tell you, not seven times but seventy times seven times." (Matt. 18:21 *ff.*) This means that forgiveness is no limited duty, of which a man can acquit himself, but it results necessarily from the attitude which he is to take toward his neighbor, the attitude which knows no claim of his own.

Finally it is now clear that *love does not mean an emotion* which quickens the spiritual life and makes it sensitive, but a definite attitude of the will. Love for neighbor and enemy depends not on an emotional and sentimental feeling of pity or admiration, which finds in the most profligate individual the spark of the divine, of noble, inextinguishable humanity; rather it depends on the command of God. Love is then not an affection of peculiar strength among the feelings and affections which fill the human soul in all possible shades and varieties. If love were emotion and affection, it would be conceivable that besides love and hate there could also be a third attitude, indifference. But if love means the surrender of one's own will for the good of the

other man, in obedience to God, there exists for man
only the Either-Or of love and hate. Whoever does not
love, whoever is indifferent, is in bondage to his natural
feelings, his natural self; he lives in hate. For to do
good only to those who do good to us, to be kind only
to those who are kind to us, means acting as the sinners
and heathen also do, that is, it is the behavior of the
natural, selfish man.

In reality the love which is based on emotions of
sympathy, on affection, is self-love; for it is a love of
preference, of choice, and the standard of the preference and choice is the self. Friendship and family love
are expressions of the natural self; they are as such
neither good nor bad; they are bad when the will of the
man is bad. But to see in them the fulfillment of God's
command to love is to falsify this command and to set
self-love in the place of obedient love of neighbor. For
the neighbor is not this or that man with whom I feel
a bond of sympathy, it is every man; yet not every man
in general, but every man with whom I come in contact.
The command is, you must love; the will is called to
action, that is, the man is addressed, with the implication that he is placed by God under the necessity of
decision and must decide through his free act. Only if
love is thought of as an emotion is it meaningless to
command love; the *command* of love shows that love is
understood as an attitude of the will.

Such love is clearly neither weak nor feeble. It does

not consist in sentimental emotion, nor look upon the neighbor in his actual person as something especially precious, which must be admired or cherished. It is not the fostering of the individuality of others because of one's joy in it. For man is not seen by Jesus as "individuality" at all. He is seen as standing under the demand of God. So true love of neighbor will never indulge and weaken him, but will recognize him as also under the necessity of decision and treat him accordingly. Otherwise Jesus' call to repentance could not be understood as an act of love.

In conclusion, there is a saying of Jesus which perhaps can show how little it is possible to seek for an ethic of Jesus in the sense of an idealistic doctrine of duties and virtues, or in the sense of an ethic of goods or values; how, on the contrary, the responsibility for all concrete moral decisions is thrust upon man, and these decisions are bound up with the one Either-Or, obedience or disobedience. It is the saying, "Be perfect, as your heavenly Father is perfect." (Matt. 5:48)

The saying is of course preserved in another form, "Be merciful as your Father is merciful." (Luke 6:36) But the first form is probably the older, and was changed by Luke to make a transition to the following section. However, in order to understand the saying we must consider—on the assumption that it is genuine, and therefore spoken not in Greek but in Aramaic— that it is not allowable to introduce here the Greek idea of perfection. For the Greeks, perfection is the ideal, the highest possibility of conduct, to be attained by gradual improvement; the perfect is the pinnacle of all relative values. That would not be consistent with Jesus' view of God, according to which God does not stand in direct relation to relative values. Neither does this Greek view correspond at all to the Semitic conception of "perfect," which is an absolute conception. The latter means "sound," "whole"; applied to man, it can also mean "exact," "true." In this way must Jesus' words be understood; they assert that the conduct of man should be whole and undivided, not this and that together; true and exact, unwavering, no running back and forth. And this requirement is based on the reference to God Himself, with whom also there is only the Either-Or, not Both-And. This saying expresses the whole emphasis of the demand of Jesus; man stands in the crisis of decision, and this decision is not something relative, a stage of his development, but the Either-Or before which God has placed him, so that the man's decision has final character; he becomes thereby a righteous man or a sinner.

Again the question arises, is this requirement not impossible? And what if the man is a sinner?

8. *The Will of God and the Coming of His Kingdom*

Before we enter upon this question, there is still one thing to consider. How is the preaching of Jesus concerning the will of God related to his proclamation of the coming of the Kingdom? Or, as it could be phrased, how are Jesus the rabbi and Jesus the prophet related? This question is not intended to apply to Jesus' personality and the methods of his historical ministry, but to the content of his preaching. Is it conceivable that he who as eschatological prophet proclaims the coming of the Kingdom and drives out demons, at the same time as a rabbi teaches his disciples and enters into disputes about questions of the Law which were important at that time? In what sense do the message "The Kingdom of God is near" and the demand "Be perfect" form a unity? Indeed, are they a unity at all?

In more recent times this has been frequently disputed. It would be possible to say simply: The fulfilling of the will of God, obedience, is the *condition* for participation in the Kingdom, for entrance into it. In a certain sense this is true, yet it is not a wholly satisfactory answer. For this connection could be conceived externally; participation in the Kingdom of God might appear as the reward sought by obedience, and thus the radical character of obedience would be lost. Especially from that point of view the peculiar way in which Jesus speaks of obedience would be misunderstood. For all other possible requirements, for example the requirement of complete observance of the Law, may otherwise be thought of as the condition for entrance into the Kingdom. From a rabbi, for instance, this word is recorded: "If the Israelites should keep strictly to the Law for only two Sabbaths, they would immediately be redeemed." Jesus says nothing of this kind.

An intrinsic connection of eschatological preaching and moral demand would evidently exist only if the coming Kingdom is so conceived that it becomes clear without further explanation that there can be no other condition except the one, radical obedience. On the other hand this inner connection can exist only if in this demand for obedience nothing is involved which conflicts with the belief in the coming Kingdom, if rather the demand for obedience really coincides with the call to prepare for the future.

Since Jesus did not preach theoretical reflections, but appealed immediately to the will of the hearer, the answer to this question is not to be found directly in his words, but must be sought in the fundamental view underlying them. Indeed it seems strange at first sight that the prophet should also have been a rabbi, that interpretation of the Law and eschatological preaching should belong together. Thus it is easy to understand why many scholars have ignored or changed the meaning of the eschatological preaching of the coming Kingdom. They have understood the Kingdom as an inner spiritual possession, or as the actual fellowship of those who in obedience to God's will build by moral endeavor the Kingdom of God on earth. Both are, as we have previously shown, historical misunderstandings, and these conceptions are today almost completely abandoned.[1]

There is still another way out; the explanation has been given that the eschatological preaching does not come from Jesus. He was only a teacher of the Law, who taught a new morality, a "better righteousness." The eschatological message was first put into his mouth by the church. After his death his adherents, at first despairing, united under the lasting influence of his personality, and after they had seen him in visions as risen from the dead, they expected that he would return as the Messiah, the "Son of Man," on the clouds of heaven, and would set up the Kingdom. From their glowing hope for the future the eschatological sayings originated which were attributed to Jesus.

This is possible. Yet if it were true, the meaning of the eschatological message would still be fundamentally the same, and the question would still remain whether and how this message and the preaching of the will of God were combined into a unity in the early church. Instead of the preaching of Jesus the preaching of the early church would call for explanation, and since the investigation really concerns the content, meaning, and validity for us of what is taught in the gospels, the question of how much the historical Jesus and how much other people have contributed to that content is of secondary importance.

[1] Professor Bultmann is of course speaking for German theologians.

This is possible. But it is historically **extremely improbable**. For the certainty with which the Christian community puts the eschatological preaching into the mouth of Jesus is hard to understand if he did not really preach it. Further, the critical analysis of the text shows that later sayings have often been added to an older eschatological stratum, and these later editions exhibit characteristic interests of the church, for example the interest in the dignity of their leaders and the rewarding of the faithful (Matt. 19:27, 28, or Luke 22:28, 29; Mark 10:28–30), or the anxiety over the delayed coming of the "Son of Man" (Luke 12:35–38, 47–48; Mark 13:31, 33–37), or threats of punishment against the unbelieving Jews. (*Cf.* Matt. 11:21–24, Luke 19:39–44, 23:28–31) It is probable that such sayings as betray no church interests at all really go back to Jesus. Finally, the movement which Jesus started, his entry into Jerusalem, and his death on the cross, are historically comprehensible only if he really spoke as a Messianic prophet. Indeed he was probably far more an eschatological prophet than is apparent from the tradition.

It is then natural that other scholars have thought just the opposite, that he was *only* an eschatological prophet, and either that his preaching of the will of God is to be understood only in the light of the eschatology, or that it does not come from him at all but was ascribed to him by the church. When after his death

the first turbulent movement subsided and his adherents
united to form a community, they came more and more
into conflict with orthodox Judaism, from which they
had separated. From this time come the disputes over
interpretation of the Law, in which they appealed to the
authority of Jesus and represented him as the rabbi
which he had never been.

This too is extremely improbable. In one point only
is it correct, that in fact the community separated more
and more from orthodox Judaism, that the disputes
between Jesus and his opponents were now recounted
and written down as models, and were naturally told in
such a way as to correspond to the interests of the
church. Doubtless, then, without critical scrutiny some
words were attributed to Jesus which had originated in
the community, in controversy with opponents or in the
interests of closer organization of the church. Probably most of the sayings where proof texts are used in
argument took shape first in the community (*cf.* Matt.
9:13; 12:5, 6, 7; Mark 7:6, 7; 12:26, 27); likewise
certain directions for the life of the church. (Matt.
5:17–19; 18:15–17, 19, 20, etc.)

But against the supposition that all words of Jesus
about the Law and the requirement of God originated
in the community, there are two decisive reasons. First
there is the fact that the community saw in Jesus the
Messiah, and expected his coming in Messianic glory.
It is incredible that they would transform into a rabbi

him whom they looked upon as Messiah. For stories to be told of him as a rabbi, the picture of his actual work as a teacher of the Law must have been distinctly impressed on their memory; later it was gradually thrust into the background by the figure of the Messiah. Further we know that the primitive church held fast to the Law with great fidelity; it did not understand the double edge of certain of the sayings of Jesus about the Law, and in opposition to Paul and other Hellenistic Christian missionaries maintained firmly the ideal of legalistic perfection. It is then incredible that the words of Jesus which in their implications shatter this ideal and destroy the spirit of legalism originated in the church; they must go back to Jesus himself. Of course in many special cases we cannot be certain what comes from the community and what from Jesus. But we cannot doubt that the most important sayings, which demand radical obedience to the will of God, go back to Jesus.

There is one more expedient which has often been tried: the words of Jesus about the will of God are to be understood strictly in the light of the eschatological message. That is in a certain sense entirely correct, but here it has a special meaning which remains to be tested. The eschatological message is taken one-sidedly to mean the prediction of the dramatic events of the end of the age, the prediction of the destruction of the world. It is argued that because of this expectation of the imminent end of the world, Jesus had no interest in the different aspects of moral life, in marriage and work, in the value of property and civil order. He did not intend to give absolute rules for man's conduct; his ethic was an "interim-ethic," that is, his commands were only practical rules for the last short span of time which remained before the end. For this brief time one must do his utmost, enlist all his energy.

Now it is certainly true that as a result of the expectation of the imminent end of this world, Jesus was not interested in many of the concrete possibilities in which man's obedience can be proved on earth. But this does not mean that obedience is merely relative, a matter of prudent rules for attaining a share in the Kingdom, rather than radical and absolute. We need only remember that eschatological expectation in itself is not necessarily associated with the call to repentance and with the preaching of the will of God. It can be combined just as well with wishful fantasies of future glory, with economic ideals and hopes, with thoughts of revenge and pictures of hell. Jewish apocalyptic as well as the history of eschatology elsewhere offers abundant proof of this. It still needs to be explained why such ideas are not found with Jesus and why, on the contrary, with him the demand for obedience goes hand in hand with the proclaiming of the future age.

Moreover Jesus' sayings about the will of God in detail show very clearly that they are by no means meant as interim-ethic. We need only compare with Jesus' teaching on the will of God a prophecy of the prophet Jeremiah in order to see the difference.

"A word of Yahweh came to me:
Take no wife for yourself,
no son shall you have,
no daughters in this place,
for thus has Yahweh spoken
against the sons and daughters
who are born in this place,
and against the mothers who bore them
and against their fathers who begat them.
Through the plague shall they die,
perish by sword and by famine,
become dung on the face of the ground,
with none to mourn and none to bury them.
They belong to the birds of heaven
and to the beasts of the earth.

"So has Yahweh spoken:
Enter not into a house where they cry woe,
go not to the mourning,
put on no mourning garments,
for I have taken my blessing from this people.
No one will lament over them and tear himself,
no one let his hair be cut for their sakes,
no one break bread for a mourner
to comfort him for his dead,
nor give him to drink from the beaker of comfort,
for his father or his mother.

"Go not into a house where a banquet is held,
to sit with them at food and drink,
for so hath Yahweh spoken:
Take care, I bring to silence in this place

before your eyes, in your days,
song of joy and song of rejoicing,
song of the bride and the bridegroom."

(Jer. 16:1–9)

Here we see plainly how the behavior of the prophet, his renunciation of marriage, of participation in the mourning for the dead and the festal joy of his people, is not based on the absolute demand for obedience but on the vision of the approaching catastrophe. It is otherwise with Jesus; for neither in the condemning of legalistic piety nor in the requirements of the Sermon on the Mount does reference to the imminent end of the world play any part whatever. Hypocrisy is rebuked without the threat of hell fire; love of enemies is demanded without the promise of heavenly joys. Altogether the will of God is complete obedience, surrender of one's own claim. There can therefore be no question of an interim-ethic, of relative requirements by which the claim of man is merely deferred for awhile. It is true however that Jesus' demands are in one point to be understood in the light of the eschatological message—namely that in them "Now" appears as the decisive hour.

This leads us to see *how truly the eschatological message and the preaching of the will of God are to be comprehended as a unity.* It should first be noted that in the great prophets of the Old Testament and the great prophet of Iran, Zarathustra, a similar association of

129

eschatology and moral demand is found. It can be easily understood that the prophet, in the consciousness of having freshly and clearly discerned the will of God, would look upon the unhappy earthly conditions as ripe for destruction and preach an overturning of all things by a mighty catastrophe. But if we seek so to explain the preaching of Jesus, we should have only a psychological explanation, not an insight into the inner relationship of eschatology and demand.

Rather we should say: the difficulty in grasping this connection as a unity really arises because both the eschatology and the demand are not understood in their final decisive sense. So long as we speak of an ethic of Jesus in the usual sense, we cannot understand how the teacher of a system of ethics can at the same time preach the imminent end of everything in the world. For a system of ethics presupposes the existence of the world and of the human race under the conditions of this world as they are known to us. It presents ideals, or at least ends, which are to be realized by our action, and at the same time a future which is under our control. All this is expressly denied in the eschatological message of Jesus; he knows no ends for our conduct, only God's purpose; no human future, only God's future. But so we have learned to understand Jesus' preaching of the will of God. In it no ends were prescribed for man, no future placed under his control. Every ideal of personality or of society, every ethic of values and

goods was repudiated. The one concern in this teaching was that man should conceive his immediate concrete situation as the decision to which he is constrained,
and should decide in this moment for God and surrender his natural will. Just this is what we found to
be the final significance of the eschatological message,
that man *now* stands under the necessity of decision,
that his "Now" is always for him the last hour, in which
his decision against the world and for God is demanded,
in which every claim of his own is to be silenced. Since,
then, the message of the coming of the Kingdom and
that of the will of God point men to *the present moment as the final hour* in the sense of the hour of decision, the two do form a unity, each is incomplete
without the other.

For the Kingdom of God remains a dark and silent
entity, like death, as long as it is not plain that the demand for decision has for man a clear, comprehensible
meaning. Only then is the determination of the present
by the future Kingdom not a denial of the present but
its fulfillment; only so is the future a controlling factor
in the present.

Conversely, the will of God, as calling man in the
present to decision, is comprehensible only if this will
gives man a future. For this decision is no choice between two possibilities which lie equally at man's disposal; it is a true crisis, that is, the Either-Or between
two possibilities, in which the "old man" leaves his po-

sition of independence and comes under the sovereignty of another. The sovereign in both cases is God, either the angry, judging God, or the gracious God. A man becomes through the decision either a sinner or righteous. The *real* future stands before man in decision, not the false future over which he already has control, but the future which will give him a character which he does not yet have. This is the meaning of the present instant, that it involves the necessity of decision because it leads into the future.

Then the question becomes all the more urgent: How does it stand with the sinner? Is there still a future for him? Can there be one, if he is condemned by God? Can the freedom of decision for man be repeated? Or does not the seriousness of the last hour mean that the decision is final?

IV

The Teaching of Jesus: God the Remote and the Near

1. The Jewish Conception of God

Here once more, in order to understand Jesus' conception of God we must show its connection with the Jewish conception, at the same time differentiating between them. The distinguishing peculiarity common to both conceptions is at once clear when we contrast them with the modified conception of the Jews who were, like those in Alexandria, under the influence of Greek philosophy. There God is thought of under the concepts of law and of ideal. This corresponds to Greek thinking. For the Greek it is in the first place axiomatic that God, like other objects of the world, can be examined by the thinking observer; that there can be a theology in the exact, immediate sense. That Judaism has no such theology is due not to any incapacity or lack of development in its thought, but to the fact that Judaism has from the beginning a different conception of God; He does not in any sense belong to the world of objects about which man orients himself through thought.

One should not in this connection let himself be deceived by the observation that the abstract thinking of the Greeks made it possible for them to understand in its purity the essence of the spiritual, and that therefore mythological, anthropomorphic ideas of God were abandoned by the Greeks, while in Judaism naïve mythological and anthropomorphic expressions about God, although they decrease, do not by any means disappear. In reality, Greek thought always regards God in the last analysis as a part of the world or as identical with the world, even when, or rather especially when, He is held to be the origin and formative cosmic principle which lies beyond the world of phenomena. For here, too, God and the world form a unity within the grasp of thought; the meaning of the world becomes clear in the idea of God. Greek thought tends therefore to pantheism, which finds its final and most impressive embodiment in the Stoic philosophy. God appears as the law ruling in the universe which gives form to all phenomena—law which differs from the modern "natural law" because it is not wholly and essentially defined by the concept of cause and effect, but rather by the concept of a creative, active, form-giving power. Such a representation of God corresponds to the conception which the Greek man had of himself as a microcosm, receiving form from a law identical with the great cosmic law, a form which is present as an ideal norm in human will and knowledge.

To the different conception of man which dominates

Judaism (this has been previously discussed), there corresponds *a wholly different conception of God.* As man is here seen to be essentially a being who wills, so God is primarily Will, and moreover sovereign, uncaused Will, which has no need to justify the willing on any rational grounds before the bar of intellect. In His *relation to the world* God is not the first principle, the origin, intelligible to the intellect, from which the existence of the world can be deduced; not the formative power which is immanent in all its manifestations, not the law of the world, but the creating Will. He commands, and it happens; He decrees, and it exists. (Psalm 33:9) For His glory He created the world, and all His works must praise Him.

"They all wait for Thee,
that Thou mayest give to them in due season.
Thou givest to them, they gather it,
Thou openest Thine hand, they are satisfied with good
    things.
Thou hidest Thy face, they are terrified;
Thou takest away their breath, they perish
and return to the dust, which they were.
Thou sendest forth Thy breath, they are created,
and Thou makest new the face of the earth."
                                        (Psalm 104:27–30)

God is the Creator: this does not mean that He gave form to some already existing matter, but that He created the world according to His will. In later Judaism this idea is developed to entire clarity, and it is

135

expressly said that God created the world out of nothing.

In *relation to man,* God is the sovereign Lord who deals with man according to His will as the potter with the clay, Who rejects whom He will and has mercy on whom He will. His will has prescribed for man what is good and evil. It is not an ideal, simply an expression of all that is potential in man, determining by its formative power the conduct of man. Man has only to ask what the Lord requires; he is not obliged to bring his humanity to its pure form, he must be obedient. This view finds rather crude expression in the assumption that the Law, even where it is wholly incomprehensible to man, requires obedience. There is therefore no distinction made between the physical nature in man and the spiritual, through which the lower physical nature receives its law and form. Instead the man is seen as a unity, determined by his good or evil will.

Also the Jewish idea of God is to be marked off on the negative side from any *metaphysical dualism.* To be sure, Persian dualism influenced the Jewish thought world in later times; for example, the figure of Satan is a Persian intrusion into Judaism. But the peculiar character of the Jewish concept of God, even when it does not reach full clarity, is preserved. God and the world do not stand over against each other as two hostile natures or substances. The idea of the Creator is never given up, and no inherent law or power is ever ascribed to the world; God is the Almighty, in spite of Satan to whom He permits temporary activity. And though God and man are sharply contrasted as Creator and creature, as the Holy One and the sinner, still this difference is never regarded as a difference between two natures, nor is the redemption of man conceived as deliverance from a lower and endowment with a higher nature. Genuine sacramental piety and genuine asceticism are therefore lacking in true Judaism, since the whole conception of nature which underlies metaphysical dualism is lacking. The world and man are creations of God, and hence not evil by nature; they have been corrupted by sin, and sin is not a condition of nature but the evil will of man. God is not for man something wholly alien by nature, not the "unknown"; He is the Creator, known through His Law, and is therefore the Judge.

All this does not merely present the background for Jesus' conception of God; it actually characterizes Jesus' conception. For all these characteristics are self-evident for Jesus as a Jew, and they are clearly assumed in his preaching. However, in what has been said only a negative definition has been attempted, and we must now consider more closely the positive character of the Jewish conception of God and hence also that of Jesus.

The essential element in the Jewish conception is the peculiar conjunction of the supramundane character and transcendence of God with the dependence of the world on God or with God's direction of the world; more simply expressed, the union of *the remoteness and the nearness of God*. The thought that God is remote, far above the world and man, is just as necessary an element of the idea of God as the other, that He is nevertheless constantly near. The first idea is especially emphasized in later Judaism, partly because of foreign influences, but also because monotheism became more fully developed. For in ancient Israel, although it was taken for granted that Israel could invoke one God and Lord, it was equally assumed that other nations have other gods, although Yahweh, God of Israel, is the mightiest among them. In later Judaism Yahweh is on the contrary regarded as the only existing God. And this monotheism is not, as in Greece, the result of philosophical reflection, which seeks a single origin and principle, in the interest of an intellectual understanding of the world; it is the belief in the one God which brings the concept of God itself to clear expression. For so long as a plurality of gods is accepted, the idea of God is not clearly thought; God is still a being within the universe, and many such beings are conceivable.

In Jewish monotheism it is not a philosophical world view but the belief in the transcendence of God, in God the Creator, that stands out. It is also significant that the proper name of God, Yahweh, is no longer used, for this has meaning only so long as God appears as a subject among other subjects which must be distinguished from the others by a definite name. Already in the Book of Job and in Ecclesiastes, the proper name of God is lacking. God was now designated as King and Lord, as the Most High and the Holy One, that is, by expressions which were natural to the Oriental mode of speech, and are meant to express the transcendence of God over the world and man. Other epithets indeed were chosen which were based rather on reflection, and which expressed still more strongly the remoteness of God, His distance from the world: "Heaven," "Magnificence," "Majesty," "Glory"; or in reverent awe circumlocutions were used: for example, not "God has determined," but "it was determined." Such expressions appear in many of the sayings of Jesus. (*E.g.* Luke 15:7, 10, 18; 6:38; 12:20; 16:9)

When reflective imagination, naïve or speculative, turns to the idea of God, images arise in Judaism as well as elsewhere to picture the relation of the transcendent God to the world. God was represented as an Oriental monarch, served by a retinue of angels who carried out His commands in the world; or under the influence of foreign mythology and speculation, semidivine powers were introduced who mediated between God and the world. These latter were confined to limited circles, while the belief in angels was generally accepted and was taken for granted by Jesus.

What is essential in the concept of God is not, however, the way in which His activity in the world was imaginatively conceived; what is essential is that the transcendent, remote God is at the same time near, that He holds in mighty hands the destiny of the world, of His people, and of each individual. This is brought out primarily in the idea of *creation,* which in Judaism is not a cosmological theory but the expression of the dependence of man upon God throughout his whole existence, the expression of the consciousness of being a *creature* before God. Moreover it stands out in this belief that God is the Lord of history, who directs it from its beginnings to an end according to His plan. Man does not stand lost in a cosmos remote from God, nor does he comfort himself with the thought that he is included as a member of the cosmic organism, whose rhythmic motion is determined by law. Instead, man stands according to the divine plan at a definite place among temporal events, which are directed toward a determined goal.

Hence the outlook of man is directed on the one hand toward the past, in which the "God of Abraham, Isaac, and Jacob" allotted blessings and chastenings to His people; and the individual knows that this history immediately concerns him, speaks to him, and determines his life by its instructions and consolations. On the other hand his outlook is directed toward the future, where God is guiding world events to their goal, exercises judgment, and lets His Kingdom appear. The tension between the concepts of the remote and the near God here reveals itself again, for God is God of the future and the present.

The unifying of these two ideas was never achieved in Judaism. The thought of the God of the future stands with one-sided emphasis and definite coloring so in the foreground that it is often not clear how this God can also be the Lord of the present. At this point dualistic imagery which entered from foreign countries, especially from Persia, exercises its influence. The whole course of time is divided into two epochs: the present age (to which past and present belong), and the future age in which the glory of God will appear. The more sharply this contrast is conceived, and the more glorious the future gleams, as the time when all powers hostile to God are annihilated, so much the more does the present appear as forsaken by God, as the time when Satan and his evil spirits work their will. Where then is the God of the present? Obviously this side of the concept of God is suppressed, and thereby the thought of the omnipotence of God is limited under the influence of dualism.

The whole idea of God is hence endangered; for it has lost its meaning, if God is not thought of as the Power which determines man in his present existence. And this danger becomes greater, the more God's revelation of the future is expected and longed for, the more complaint is made about the suffering of the present.

At the same time also the future becomes less a **real** future—by which is meant a future which determines the present because as *its own* future it is indissolubly connected with it. Rather the future is unrelated to the present, something which might possibly *not* be, and its not being would make no change in the present; something which is coming some time, but which so far as its essential nature is concerned could already *have been* some time; indeed the speculation is widespread that the blessings of salvation pre-exist and are already present in heaven. And on the other hand the future is still less a real future if man has it already in his control, so that it is subject to his own fantasies and wishes; that is, if he does not take seriously the truth that the future, being new, calls for the new man.

Under these conditions it is easy to understand that a real connection between the God of the future and the God of the present is often not to be found, or that if it is asserted, the prophecies in which God is looked upon as God of the *present* generally display the character of theoretical speculation. Of course it is asserted that the Creator of the world and the Judge of the world are *one,* that in the future there will be fulfilled simply what God has already decreed at the beginning of the world, that God rules all times and what happens in time, and is so far God of the present. But how far the God of the future actually rules man's present, in such a way that man in his present existence is determined by the God of the future—this does not often appear clearly. Rather, the pronouncements which speak of God's present activity are often without relation or even in contradiction both to the expectations of the future and to the estimate of the present, dualistic and pessimistic as that estimate is.

But in spite of the figure of Satan in Judaism, the belief in God's providence as permeating the occurrences of the present world was never given up. The edifying tale of old Tobit and his son Tobias shows how wonderfully God's providence guides the life of the faithful. Numerous passages praise this providence, which gives food to man and beast, which does not allow a bird to be snared without the will of heaven. Moreover the remote God is always accessible to the faithful in *prayer,* and is addressed as *Father* by the praying congregation, as well as by individual saints. Such confident faith in the God of the present is shown typically in the fifth Psalm of Solomon:

"Lord God, I will praise Thy name, full of joy,
in the midst of those who know Thy righteous judgments.
For Thou art kind and merciful, the refuge of the poor.
If I cry to Thee, Thou wilt not be silent.
For none take spoil from the mighty,
who then would take from all that Thou hast created, unless Thou gavest it?
For man and his lot are weighed by Thee,
and he obtains no more than Thou hast determined for him, O God.

In our tribulation we call upon Thee for aid,
and Thou wilt not refuse our prayer, for Thou art our
   God.
Let Thy hand not lie heavily upon us,
lest we in our need fall into sin.
And even if Thou help us not, we do not cease to come
   to Thee,
for if I hunger, I cry to Thee, O God, and Thou wilt
   give to me.
Thou feedest the birds and the fishes;
while Thou givest rain in the desert, so that grass
   springs up,
Thou providest food in the field for all animals,
and when they hunger, they raise their faces to Thee.
Kings and princes and people Thou feedest, O God,
and who is the hope of the poor and needy except Thee,
   O Lord?
Yes, Thou wilt hear, for who is kind and gracious like
   Thee?
Rejoice the souls of the poor, and open Thine hand in
   pity.
The kindness of man is niggardly and desires reward,
and if he gives twice without grumbling, it is a marvel.
But Thy gift is great, full of goodness, and rich,
and he who hopes in Thee will have no lack of good
   things.
Over the whole earth, O Lord, spread Thy mercy and
   Thy kindness."

Man stands, then, in a certain tension between present
and future, with no clear unity in his conception of
God. This tension between present and future, which
is shown in the attempt to combine hope for the future
and belief in a present providence, also appears in an-

other form—a form which allows the possibility of a unified conception of God to be more clearly seen: that is, *God is thought of as the future Judge of the present.* Primarily of course God, in so far as He is the Judge, is the God of the future. He will one day recompense men according to their deeds; then it is that

"The Age which now sleeps awakes, and the temporal
    itself passes away.
The earth gives back those who rest therein,
the dust releases those who sleep in it,
the vaults restore the souls entrusted to them.
The Most High appears on the throne of judgment.
Then comes the end,
and compassion passes away,
pity is far off,
and long-suffering is withdrawn.
My judgment alone will remain,
the truth will stand,
faith will triumph.
The reward follows,
recompense appears,
good deeds awake,
evil deeds sleep no more.
Then appears the pit of torment,
and on the other side the place of new life.
The fires of Gehenna become visible,
and on the other side the paradise of blessedness."
                            (4 Ezra 7:31–36)

The outlook of man is here directed to the future which will bring him punishment or reward. *God is just,* and already shows His justice in the fate of nations and of men; but His justice will be revealed clearly and decisively only on the judgment day. *God is also gracious and merciful,* and indeed He gives even now, full of kindness and mercy, good gifts to those who ask Him; but His mercy will be revealed fully and decisively only on the judgment day, when He will pardon those who are worthy. But what can a man expect? with what comfort himself? Who will be among the condemned, who among the graciously pardoned? Both as just and as gracious, God is essentially God of the future, and the future is wholly uncertain.

This is why the conduct of man, which should be nothing but obedience in the present moment, easily takes on the character of something accomplished for the future, and thereby loses its character of decision. It becomes a good work among other works; for the more good works there are, the more acquittal in the judgment is to be hoped for. Thus the man loses easily the consciousness of standing before God in the decisive "Now," and becomes fearful of the day when he *will* stand before God. An overwhelming *sense of sin* therefore takes possession of the religious man; his thought struggles with the problem of sin. How did sin come into the world? Whence comes its power? How is it possible that so many men should be lost? Especially in the apocalypse of 4 Ezra these questions are discussed. And from the feeling of the insecurity of salvation arise the confessions of sin and prayers of repentance which are so typical of later Judaism. Ever

and again it is repeated, "We have sinned before Thee!"
"With a broken heart and a humble spirit, may we find
acceptance." And the last refuge is to regard even this
confession of sin, this penitential prayer, as a good
work, as a means by which to insure God's grace.

"We and our fathers have lived in the works of death,
but Thou, even because we are sinners, art called Merci-
ful.
For even because we have not works of righteousness,
Thou wilt, when Thou hast compassion on us, be called
Gracious.
For the righteous, who have laid up many works with
Thee,
will receive reward for their works.
But what is man, that Thou shouldst be angry at him?
What is the race of mortals, that Thou couldst bear
resentment toward it?
For in truth there is none born of woman who sins not,
no one of those who have lived, who has not trans-
gressed;
then indeed are Thy justice and Thy kindness manifest,
O Lord,
when Thou pitiest those who have no treasure of good
works." (4 Ezra 8:31–36)

Here it is shown clearly that the *idea of sin* is not
radically conceived, so long as the idea of the possibility
of good works persists along with it, so long as the
confession of sin can be something which makes sin
pardonable, so long as man is not seen as wholly and in
everything a sinner before God. The idea of sin is not
radically conceived, if along with it there is room for

the thought: a man cannot know how great the sins are in proportion to the good works; if the thought prevails that in the future judgment good and evil works are to be weighed against each other. The uncertainty in which a man here finds himself is not the consciousness of his utter nothingness before God, but a wavering between fear and hope. The God of the future is not really God of the present; for in the present the man is still conscious of an effort to escape the judgment of God, of a possibility of justifying himself before God; he does not see himself standing in the present before the God who judges.

Likewise the idea of the *grace of God* is not radically conceived; for God's grace appears here as a kindly overlooking of sins, standing in opposition to His justice, as it were overcoming His justice. Radically thought, on the contrary the grace of God belongs inseparably with His righteous judgment; for His grace does not *ignore* sin, but *forgives* it. It is precisely to the sinner that God is gracious, that is, to him who stands condemned by His justice. God's grace is not radically thought, so long as it is conceived as a possibility in the future instead of being grasped as a reality in the present; for what right would a man have to assert the grace of God, if he did not see it revealed as a concrete reality in his own life? Otherwise he is merely representing God as a human being who will perhaps give preference to grace over justice. In the

Jewish prayer of penitence, therefore, the man who is hoping for God's pity is not comforted by laying hold of the revealed grace of God, but is consoling himself by a despairing clutch at a questionable possibility. The God of the future is not really God of the present, for the man does not see the God of grace at all in the present.

And yet precisely when God is seen as Judge and man as sinner, there is *a possibility of a unified conception of God;* a possibility of closing the chasm between God distant and God near at hand, between future and present, between hope and belief in providence. For then it is understood that the remoteness of God is nothing other than His remoteness from the sinner, and therefore a remoteness into which man is forced by the very fact that here and now he stands before God. Then it can be recognized that the need and suffering of the world are the *sinner's* need and suffering, and so do not stand in contradiction to the providence of God, and that the right to affirm the providence of God exists only for him to whom the God of the present is at the same time God of the future.

For Judaism, at all events, pessimistic dualism is endurable because in fact man is regarded as a sinner before God, and God as the Holy One and the Judge. But certainly Judaism did not achieve a really unified idea of God, because neither the idea of sin nor the idea of God's grace is radically conceived. It is not only

mental activity, clear logic, or more persistent thinking that is needed in order to conceive these ideas radically; for the concepts of sin and grace have their origin
not in theoretical reflection, they are the expression of
man's experience that the reality of his own existence is
determined by sin and grace. And this understanding
of himself does not depend on an act of thought, but is
a part of life itself.

2. The God of the Future

These observations have already set forth certain
fundamental aspects of Jesus' conception of God, and
points at which his view of God differs from the Jewish, in spite of all they have in common. Like strict
Judaism his thinking is far removed from the Greek.
God is for him in the Jewish sense *the remote God,* who
in no way belongs to the world nor is part of the world.
In certain peculiarities of expression, in the habit of
sometimes speaking of God in circumlocutions, Jesus
resembles the pious Jews, if our record is to be trusted
on this point. (Luke 15:7, 10, 18; 6:38; 12:20; 16:9)
Likewise he speaks freely of the angels, who are God's
servants. (*E.g.* Matt. 18:10, Mark 8:38, Luke 12:8, 9)
But just here his own attitude is plainly shown, for he
does not make angels and heavenly things objects of
speculation, nor impart secret information about them,
as Jewish apocalyptists speculate about the names and
duties of the angels, about the stars and the winds.

For him God is not an object of thought, of speculation; he does not press into service the concept of God
in order to understand the world and comprehend it as
a unity. Therefore God is to him neither a metaphysical entity nor a cosmic power nor a law of the universe,
but personal Will, holy and gracious Will. Jesus speaks
of God only to affirm that man is claimed by the will
of God and determined in his present existence through
God's demand, His judgment, His grace. The distant
God is at the same time *the God near at hand,* Whose
reality is not to be grasped when a man seeks to escape
from his own concrete existence, but precisely when he
holds it fast. Jesus speaks of God not in terms of general truths, in dogmas, but only in terms of what God
is for man, how He deals with man. He does not speak
objectively of the attributes of God, of His eternity,
unchangeableness, and the like, by which Greek thought
strove to describe the transcendent nature of God. He
says incidentally that God is merciful and kind (Luke
6:36, Mark 10:18) ; but in this he expresses only man's
experience of God in his own life, he speaks only of
God's dealing with man.

It is not that Jesus distinguishes between a remote,
mysterious, metaphysical *nature* of God, and God's
dealing with us as the *expression* of this nature; rather
the remote and the near God are one. It is impossible
to speak of God in Jesus' sense without speaking of His
activity. As with man, in Jesus' sense, there can be no

distinction between his nature and his actions which are the result of his nature, but the actual essence of man is present in action, likewise God is present where He is active. Jesus then does not make known a new conception of God, or revelations of the nature of God; instead, he brings the message of the coming Kingdom and of the will of God. He speaks of God in speaking of man and showing him that he stands in the last hour of decision, that his will is claimed by God.

Hence any conception of God as a higher nature is foreign to Jesus. A man cannot through cultic, sacramental means bring himself into closer relation to the remote God, nor obtain for himself a divine nature. As little as Jesus thinks of cult as a good work, does he think of it as a mysterious means of freeing man from his lower nature. The concept of nature in general is unknown to him, and nothing is for him low or evil except the evil will of man. It is not sacramental washings that make a man pure, but only a pure heart, that is, a good will. (Mark 7:15) What significance Jesus saw in John's baptism we cannot now tell. Perhaps he took it for granted that his followers, like himself, had been baptized. The later tradition that he himself baptized (John 3:22) is not reliable. Probably the baptism of John was an eschatological sacrament, and may have had in the circle of the Baptizer some peculiar sacramental meaning, but Jesus can scarcely have seen more in it than the acknowledgment of penitence before the coming of the Kingdom. Certainly he did not himself institute baptism as a sacramental means of salvation, as the legendary account in Matt. 28:19 says, and as the practice of baptism in the Hellenistic Christian churches suggests.

The Hellenistic Christians saw Jesus also as the founder of a *sacramental meal,* the Lord's Supper, and under the influence of this later view the account of the last supper of Jesus with his disciples was modified. (Mark 14: 22–25, etc.) But this is certainly an intrusion of the sacramental viewpoint of Hellenistic Christianity into the original tradition. The teaching of Jesus and that of the oldest group of his followers contained no trace of any such sacramental conception. All the presuppositions for this are lacking, that is, all ideas of an intrinsic worthlessness of human nature compared with the intrinsic worth of divine holiness.

Jesus no more teaches *a mystic relation to God* than he conceives of access to God as mediated through cult and sacrament. "Love the Lord your God with all your heart and with all your soul and with all your strength" (Mark 12:30) does not mean man's loss of himself as an independent personality, a submersion of self in the stream of divine life. Instead, this highest commandment is clearly defined, addressed to the will of man, by the second, "Love your neighbor as yourself." (Mark 12:31) The individual life of man is not annihilated in his relationship to God, but on the contrary is awakened to its own reality, because the man is constrained to decision. God Himself must vanish for the man who does not know that the essence of his own life consists in the full freedom of his decision, that through the decision of his will, through obedience, he can win fellowship with God. Otherwise God would be a universal natural substance, something non-rational; psychological experiences, excitement and ecstasy, devotion and joy, would be interpreted as communion with God. As little as Jesus describes the nature of God in these terms does he speak of spiritual states and experiences. All mystical designations of God are lacking in his teaching, and all talk of the soul and its emotional states. A mystical conception of God can be dualistic or pantheistic, or even both in some peculiar combination.

Just as none of these tendencies are to be found with Jesus, because for him God is visible in His will and activity, so there is no trace of a corresponding conception of man. For Jesus man is not a cosmic being, in whose body and spirit the forces of the divine nature flow and are active, a microcosm and mirror of the divine in miniature. Jesus neither distinguishes sense and spirit, lower and higher, in man, nor does he speak of the divine which is confined in the prison of the body and must be released so that it can free itself from the material and be united with God. The man is wholly evil if his eye is not single, if his heart is not pure, if his will is not obedient. Always a man is conceived only as standing before God, constrained to a decision of will; God is the Will which demands obedience from men.

In this rejection of sacrament and mysticism, Jesus stands within the limits of strict Judaism, and differs from it not because he presents especially original ideas about God and the world, but because he apprehends the Jewish conception of God in its purity and consistency. With the same sureness with which he repudiates all apocalyptic or eschatological speculations, he holds fast to the idea that man stands before God under the necessity of decision. This becomes still clearer when we observe how for Jesus God is God of the future and God of the present, and when we ask whether and how Jesus combines these two ideas into a unity.

Jesus' God is God of the future, and with Jesus as in Judaism this conception seems to be influenced by the dualistic view of time, which regards the present as the age of corruption. In the petition "Thy Kingdom come" (Matt. 6:10), God's rule is evidently seen as not yet sovereign in the present; His name is not yet hallowed, His will is not yet done on earth as it is in heaven. If Jesus believed that he then saw the demons fleeing before the name of the Kingdom of God, and Satan put to flight, clearly he thought that until then the world was under the rule of Satan and his evil spirits. It would signify little to say against this interpretation that Jesus did not apparently adopt the phrasing "present and future age." (This is found only in sayings whose genuineness is very doubtful.) And also it would not be a weighty argument that Jesus does not, like other religious Jews, look in suspense and anxious longing into the uncertain future, but is convinced that even now the turning point of the times is at hand, and the powers of the imminent Kingdom can already be discerned. For the emphasis on immediacy does not show a fundamental difference from the dualistic judgment of the world. The world as it has hitherto existed would still not be seen in the light of the omnipotence of God; there would still not be clearly grasped a conception of God which excludes the thought that there can be a world or a time in which God does not rule. It would be implied that besides God there are other powers with which man under some circumstances must reckon.

It is also not sufficient to say that Jesus' concept of God was no philosophical theory (true as that is), and that his belief in God as the cause of all that happens did not, in Jesus' undeveloped thought, untrained in logical consistency, exclude the assumption of other active causes of world events; that the strength of Jesus' faith in God is shown precisely in his holding fast, in spite of the belief in Satan, to the thought of God as the final cause of all events. This interpretation is indeed approximately true; but all depends on rightly understanding the uniqueness of Jesus' belief in God.

For if this belief is a preconceived, rigid assumption, on the basis of which, against all experience, it is asserted that God is the final cause of all that happens, then it would clearly be true that the conception of God was not fully developed by Jesus. For his thought of God is not a general affirmation that God is the final cause of all occurrences, but the assertion that He is the Power which determines man in his concrete reality. If a man must say that he cannot find God in the reality of his own present life, and if he would compensate for this by the thought that God is nevertheless the final cause of all that happens, then his belief in God will be a theoretical speculation or a dogma; and however great the force with which he clings to this belief, it will not be true faith, for faith can be only the recognition of the activity of God in his own life. Such a man would then be fleeing from his own individual existence, in which alone he can find God, and would be consoling himself by the belief that God may be somewhere else; but then faith in God has become a will-o'-the-wisp. The conception of the rule of Satan and the remoteness of God from the present can be unified with the idea of God only if this very remoteness of God, this abandonment to Satan, is really a determination by God Himself. But whether and how this may be thought can be shown only by further discussion.

At any rate real understanding of the problem is precluded if the futurity of the Kingdom is minimized, as by the supposition that belief in the coming Kingdom is based on the firm foundation of belief in the creation, and that the Kingdom of God is simply the consummation of the creation. For the belief in God as the Creator is thereby made a theoretical idea, a general truth, which is used as an established presupposition. But the Jewish belief in creation does not possess the character of a theory to explain the universe; instead, it is the expression of the consciousness that man in his whole existence in the world is dependent upon God. It does not therefore draw conclusions concerning the present situation of men from a theoretically reasonable idea of the cosmos, but it gains understanding of the universe from a comprehension of man's own situation.

The intrusion of the Hellenistic idea of development into the views of Jesus is especially conspicuous when the Kingdom is called the consummation of the creation, so that an ascending line is drawn from the beginning to the end. In that case the Kingdom would be already present in germ in the creation, and the Kingdom would be the unfolding of these potentialities. Then ideally the Kingdom would already exist in the present, and its purely future character would be destroyed. But there can be no doubt that according to Jesus' thought the Kingdom is the marvellous, new, wholly other, the opposite of everything present. Jesus never thought of bringing the idea of the coming of the Kingdom into connection with the idea of creation.

The only connection which would be possible for his thought would be that which is here and there expressed in Jewish apocalyptic, namely, that in the blessed time of the end the first age of creation, with Paradise and its felicity, will return. This would not be a consummation of the creation, but its re-creation after it has been corrupted by the sin of men. This thought would be consistent with the view of Jesus; for here the future character of the Kingdom, its wonder and newness, would be preserved. Yet no words of such import are recorded from Jesus; and such a way of thinking is foreign to him because of its fantastic and mythological form, however congruous the underlying idea would be.

Thus if we wish to understand the message of Jesus, it is not possible to ignore the future character of the Kingdom of God nor to minimize the distance of God in the present. Instead, it is only possible to accept the paradox that the remote, future God is at the same time, precisely *because* He is the remote and future God, also God of the present. Or better, it is possible only to ask whether and how the recorded assertions of God's presence can be reconciled with the thought of the God of the future. In what sense did Jesus speak of the God of the present?

3. *Belief in the Providence and Justice of God*

Among Jesus' words there are many sayings which imply a childlike belief in providence and a naïve optimism in his view of nature and the world.

"Therefore I tell you,
Care not for your life, what you are to eat,
nor for your body, what you are to wear.
Is not living more than food,
and the body more than clothing?
Look at the ravens, they neither sow nor reap,
they have neither granaries nor barns, yet God feeds
    them.
You are much more than the birds.
Look at the lilies, they do not spin nor weave,
and yet I tell you Solomon in all his splendor was not
    robed like one of them.
If God so clothes the grass of the field, which grows
    today and tomorrow is thrown into the fire,
how much more you, O you of little faith!
Therefore do not strive for food and drink,
and do not ask too much,
for after all such things the peoples of the world strive,
but your Father knows that you need them."
           (Luke 12:22–31, or Matt. 6:25–32)

"Are not two sparrows sold for a penny?
And not one of them falls to the ground without your
    Father.
The hairs of your head are all counted,
so fear not, you are worth much more than sparrows."
           (Matt. 10:29–31, or Luke 12:6–7)

"He makes His sun rise over evil and good
and makes it rain on just and unjust." (Matt. 5:45)

These words present difficult literary and exegetical problems. According to their form they belong to the class of proverbs found in the Jewish and in all Oriental wisdom literature. According to their content, too, they belong to it, and they contain, taken by themselves, nothing characteristic of Jesus' preaching. There is therefore a serious critical question whether these and other proverbial sayings which are recorded among the words of Jesus were really spoken by him. For the most part, in the connection in which they are recorded, they are used in a specific sense which the context gives them. But since this context was created by the evangelists, it is impossible now to determine whether or how Jesus used such words, especially as most of them have numerous parallels in Jewish literature.

Yet their specific meaning must be carefully considered. For at least Jesus would not have repudiated such ideas, since they are consistent with the typically Jewish belief in God, which in general served as the basis for Jesus' thought of Him. In any case only an exact understanding of the meaning can show how the idea of God expressed in them is related to the belief in the God of the future—whether these affirmations can really stand together with the eschatological faith, or whether tradition is entirely mistaken in including them among the sayings of Jesus.

A similar belief in providence is expressed in the fifth psalm of Solomon already quoted and is found also in the Psalter; a belief in God

"Who covers the heaven with clouds,
provides rain for the earth,
makes the grass grow on the hills,
gives food for the cattle,
to the young ravens when they cry to Him."

(Psalm 147:8-9)

"Who gives the mountains drink from His stores
so that the earth is satisfied with the moisture of heaven,
who makes the grass grow for the cattle,
and plants for men that they may get food from the
    earth." (Psalm 104:13-14)

This view does not rest on the conception of *a law of life permeating nature*. It is characteristically different from any pantheistic view of nature, such as Schleiermacher for example represents, which assumes that the modern world has progressed beyond Jesus' childish view of nature, that we have succeeded in penetrating deeper into the understanding of nature than Jesus could have done. This "deeper insight" consists in seeing in the spectacle of change which nature presents, the supremacy of life, which draws even apparent death into the process of change to generate new life; so that not only in all changing phenomena but in existence itself the work of the spirit, of deity, is revealed. Such a conception is in no sense, as compared with the view-

point of these sayings of Jesus, further developed or
more profound; rather it results from a wholly different
premise, a wholly different conception of God and man;
it is based on the concept of law, æsthetically applied,
which is entirely alien to Judaism and to Jesus. In fact
a similar point of view is found in the Stoic philosophy,
formulated in a way which reminds one of the saying
in Matt. 5 :45. Seneca says:

"If you would imitate the gods, do good deeds even
to the undeserving. For the sun rises even for crimi-
nals, the seas lie open even to pirates. . . . No law can
be given to the falling rain, that it should not water the
fields of the wicked and vicious."

This thought of the uniform working of nature is far
removed from Judaism and Jesus. In the Stoic philosophy, "providence" means nothing more than the teleo-
logical character which can be discerned in the working
of natural law. Judaism and Jesus lack both the abstract idea of teleology and that of providence, and
have no word for either. The belief in providence
which is here meant does not proceed from a general
conception of nature and human life, in order to comfort the individual with the thought that in his life, too,
this purposive law prevails. Instead it proceeds from
the experiences of the individual in his own life. This
belief in providence is therefore not threatened by the

reversal of emphasis which is possible to the idea of law, and which comes to expression in Goethe's words:

"Denn unfühlend ist die Natur;
Es leuchtet die Sonne über Böse und Gute,
Und dem Verbrecher glänzen wie dem Besten
    der Mond und die Sterne."[1]

But of course this faith in providence is assailed by quite another question, with which the idea of law could adequately deal in its own way—the question of *suffering,* of the justice of God, of His righteousness in the ordering of the world. The question is really whether this idea of providence, arising from the experience of man in his actual existence, is consistent with the whole of this experience. Is it not an unjustified optimism to see only the good in the world? Is not the reality of man's life characterized by struggle and anxiety? Do not struggle and destruction prevail also in the world of plants and animals? Do not innumerable ravens and sparrows starve? Do the sun and rain come to the just and the unjust only for good and not also for harm? Is not this belief in providence, then, a piece of childish innocence, which has not yet reached maturity and has not yet opened its eyes to the misery and suffering of life? Perhaps, too, it is an example of typical Oriental lack of ambition and contentment with life.

[1] "For Nature is unfeeling:
The sun shines on the evil and the good,
And over the worst as over the best
Glitter the moon and the stars."

Actually the words taken alone, that is, apart from the rest of the teaching of Jesus, mean little more than this Oriental attitude. They then fit consistently into the proverbial literature of the east. But if they are taken in connection with the sayings of Jesus—irrespective of whether they were really spoken by him or were brought into this context by the church—they do not acquire a different meaning, but they are counterbalanced by other sayings in which the reality of man's life is discerned with a deeper seriousness. We must then recognize that these words contain nothing peculiar to Jesus, but were taken over unreflectively from the popular conception of God, either by Jesus or by the church. But the inclusion of these sayings is not due to a misconception; on the contrary, the fact that such inclusion was possible throws light on a characteristic aspect of the teaching of Jesus; and in this connection the critical question of whether or not Jesus spoke these words loses its meaning. For even if we hesitate to conceive of Jesus the eschatological prophet, the proclaimer of the will of God and repentance, as an Oriental sage, and if we do not accept such proverbs as characteristic of his message, yet the incorporation of such sayings into the message is an indication of how Jesus' belief in God should be understood. That is to say, the possibility of asking certain questions about God and of holding certain ideas about Him lies quite outside the range of ideas within which Jesus moves.

And here belongs especially the *problem of suffering,* or of the *justice of God.* That this question is not formulated is by no means under all circumstances a sign of undeveloped thinking or of an immature, childish understanding of human existence; it can also be the sign of a very different interpretation of human life which is the reverse of childish. The religion of the Old Testament and of later Judaism by no means ignored the suffering which is the lot of man, with which his existence is bound up. Its view is of course different from that of a man of a more highly developed civilization, who lives far removed from nature and far from the struggle with the powers of nature. In fact the life of the east, of the Israelite and Jewish nation, was lived much nearer to nature than that of the modern man. But that certain sayings of Oriental wisdom and of the psalms make an immediate appeal to the modern man is due to the fact that this religion has recognized clearly and taken account of a reality which modern thinking gladly ignores or seeks to evade with various theories—the reality of death, of mortality. Judaism sees that human existence emerges from mysterious darkness and is again swallowed up by it. It therefore speaks not of "nature" but of God, and God is the inscrutable Power in whose hands is the fate of man.

"Yes, man is as grass,
he blooms like the flower of the field;

if a breath of wind passes over it,
it is gone; and its place knows it no more."
(Psalm 103:15, 16)

"We must away
like the budding grass,
in the morning it buds and blossoms,
at night it withers away." (Psalm 90:5, 6)

"All flesh is like grass
and all its glory like the flower of the field;
the grass dries up, the flowers wither,
if the breath of God passes over them." (Isaiah 40:6, 7)

"Man, who is born of woman,
has few days, yet enough of pain,
like the flowers he grows and withers,
he flees away like the shadows and abides not."
(Job 14:1, 2)

This religion has also felt deeply the sorrow of life, whose pomp is naught but affliction and vanity (Psalm 90:10), and the varying, enigmatic game of fate with men. A naïve theory of the justice of God developed so far as to assert that what a man deserves happens to him; God rewards the good and punishes the wicked. But this idea could not be upheld in the face of the realities of life. A resigned acceptance of fate, as shown especially in Ecclesiastes, is the conclusion of "wisdom"; everything happens as it must, man should enjoy whatever he has, finally all is vanity. This belief in fate can also, as in the book of Job, attain deep pathos and become silence before the all-powerful, inscrutable God:

"Will the fault-finder quarrel with the Almighty?
Let an accuser of God reply!
—Truly I am too small, what am I to answer Thee?
I lay my hand upon my mouth." (Job 40:2, 4)

The motives of confident optimism and of resignation appear side by side in the wisdom literature; no reconciliation is found. Man indeed looks upon his life and his fate with a naïve demand for happiness, and if his demand is granted he is thankful and praises God's goodness; but he acquiesces if God wills otherwise. He does not claim an insight into fate nor console himself with the thought of universal law and the cosmic purpose. Instead, he holds fast on the one hand to the conviction that man has his own existence and is not a mere link of the cosmos, and on the other hand he sees that fatality, transitoriness, and insecurity belong to the essence of his life.

The question of the justice of God in the universal sense, as the Greeks formulated it, cannot arise here. Man does not see himself as a special case of the general and comfort himself thereby. Precisely because he sees insecurity and fatality as essential to human existence, he does not think of separating himself from the physical world and distinguishing within himself between a higher spiritual being and a lower physical nature. Hence admiration and wonder at the inexhaustible life forces of nature is as wholly lacking as the typically modern horror of blind nature against which spiritual, personal life rebels in vain. There is no belief in the inner superiority of spirit over nature, no conception of struggle between spirit and nature, nor of the inner growth which man can win in the battle with nature; there is lacking also the specifically modern pessimistic estimate of the world such as has received poetic expression from Strindberg or Spitteler.

Now from Jesus there are recorded, besides the affirmations of optimistic belief in providence, also a series of sayings exemplifying the attitude of resignation, for example:

"The foxes have holes
and the birds of the heaven nests,
but man has not where to lay his head." (Matt. 8:20)

"Who of you by thought can add a foot to his growth?"
(Matt. 6:27)

"Every day has sorrow enough of its own."
(Matt. 6:34b)

"To him who has, is given,
and from him who has not, is taken what he has."
(Mark 4:25)

"How does it help a man to gain the whole world and
lose his life?
What can a man give in exchange for his life?"
(Mark 8:36, 37)

It is of less significance to know how many of such optimistic or resigned "wisdom" sayings were really spoken by Jesus, than to see that the view of man set forth in this proverbial wisdom is in general accepted by Jesus. In any case no word is preserved which treats suffering as a problem. Jesus is unconscious of any question regarding the justice of God. It is significant that the early Christian church was soon disturbed by this problem, and sought to solve it by the aid partly of the Old Testament doctrine of retribution, partly of Greek philosophical ideas. Both ways are equally alien to Jesus.

We have seen that Jesus does not use the idea of reward in connection with divine justice. He is equally far from recognizing a claim on the part of man that his lot should be comprehensible and acceptable to him. He has given man no illuminating explanation of human suffering, not even of his own. For the predictions of the passion, which represent his suffering and death as willed by God and necessary to salvation, were put in his mouth subsequently by the church. If he really on the night of his betrayal spoke the prayer "Not as I will, but as Thou wilt," these words expressly deny the justice of God and signify silent submission to God like the words in the poem of Job. That suffering gives reason for doubt of the power of God, Jesus did not believe. This would have been irreconcilable with his idea of God, for the doubt presupposes that man in himself has a claim upon God and possesses a criterion by which to judge what is fitting for God and what is not. In the thought of Jesus the only doubt which has significance is the doubt which refers to man himself and shakes his natural security, the doubt which makes clear to man that he stands in the last hour, in the crisis of decision.

Here the attitude of Jesus differs from that of the wisdom literature. He did not change or develop further its ideas; the attitude of the sage is for him subordinate and incidental. He sees man as "wisdom" sees him, not as a member of the law-abiding cosmos, not as a special case of the universal, not as a dual being, composed of body and spirit, but as a unified individual with his own claims. But although the resigned attitude toward fate thrusts these claims of man into the background, Jesus has a far greater right to do so, since to him God is not merely fate but at the same time the holy Will which claims the will of man, requires his obedience. Then there is no place for the view of man as merely enduring his fate; he stands responsible under the necessity of decision.

It may be asked how from this standpoint the question of fate, of suffering, is to be answered. Jesus apparently did not consider it, or had no desire to discuss it. There can be no doubt however what the answer must be, according to the thought of Jesus, in view of his ideas of God and his conception of man. If every situation for man is one of decision, in which he must render obedience, so also is the hour of suffering; then also he must renounce his own claim—not indeed in resignation, but in an active assent to the will of God, who is God of the future and gives the future. The question of the justice of God cannot arise; for it belongs to another sphere of thought about God and man.

4. *Belief in Miracles*

The paradox of belief in the remote God who is also near is further shown in Jesus' belief in miracles. Jesus naturally shared with his contemporaries the belief that there are miracles. And this was no diluted, traditional belief in miracles, according to which events in themselves natural are called miracles on account of their significance or their surprising or terrifying character. Nor was it the attitude of pantheistic romanticism, which regards natural events, and especially all religious experiences, as in themselves miraculous. But in Jewish thought an event which is contrary to nature, which occurs outside of the known and ordinary chain of cause and effect, is called a miracle and ascribed to a supernatural cause, to the act of either God or demons; for Satan as well as God can work miracles. If a pitcher never becomes empty, if an old woman bears a child, if iron floats—these are miracles; if five thousand men are fed with five loaves and two fishes, if a sick man is healed by laying on of hands and a single word—these are miracles. Hence miracles are events which in themselves have no religious character, but which are attributed to divine (or dæmonic) causation, and this presupposes a certain conception of God.

The Christian community was convinced that *Jesus had performed miracles,* and told a good many miracle stories about him. Most of the wonder tales contained in the gospels are legendary, at least they have legendary embellishments. But there can be no doubt that Jesus did the kind of deeds which were miracles to his mind and to the minds of his contemporaries, that is, deeds which were attributed to a supernatural, divine cause; undoubtedly he healed the sick and cast out demons. However decidedly he refused the demand to prove his claim by a miracle (Mark 8:11, 12), he obviously himself understood his miracles as a sign of the imminence of the Kingdom of God (Luke 11:20, Mark 3:27, Matt. 11:5), exactly as his church was later convinced that it possessed the powers of the Messianic age to work miracles (Acts 2:43, 4:9–12, etc.), and as his disciples believed that they performed miracles in his name. (Mark 6:7, 2 Cor. 12:12)

It is equally clear that Jesus did not, like the later apologists, think of miracles as a proof for the existence and rule of God; for he knew no doubt of God. Miracle indeed presupposes belief in God. Therefore Jesus puts no special stress on his miracles, and at any rate is never greedy for miracles and does not, like other ancient and modern Messiahs, revel in his power of performing them.

There is no great value in investigating more closely how much in the gospel miracle tales is historical; nor is much importance to be attached to determining how far we should today consider the deeds of Jesus as miracles—that is, refer them directly to a divine cause. It is extremely worth while to emphasize that to represent this divine causality after the analogy of natural law and to speculate upon the laws of supernatural activity in the spiritual world is to mistake entirely Jesus' belief in miracle. For Jesus applied the idea of law neither to God nor to the world, and his concept of causality is not abstract but concrete, referring a specific phenomenon to a specific cause, as daily experience taught him.

Fundamental in the thought of Jesus is the conception of man as a being whose every action arises out of intention, out of will. Originally primitive man, like a child, ascribes definite intentions also to the objects of his environment, natural objects. The repetitions of everyday experiences lead him to forget this assumption, and then he inquires into an intention behind events only when it is a question of occurrences out of the ordinary, which are for him "wonderful," "miraculous." He does not assume the causality of a higher law, but the causality of a definite intention, of a will, which, since it is not human, must be divine or dæmonic. Jesus' belief in miracles, then, does not mean that Jesus was convinced of special supernatural forces and laws, but simply that he held certain happenings to be the direct action of God, that he attributed particular events in an especial sense to the will of God.

The peculiar problem of Jesus' belief in miracles is the question of its relation to his idea of God. How can God be the Almighty, the Power Who determines all, Who is active in every event, while at the same time single events are ascribed in an especial sense to His will? Does not the belief in miracle nullify the idea of omnipotence? If special occurrences are distinguished from everyday happenings as the activity of God, does this not presuppose that in general God is *not* active? Is not the same dualism revealed here as in the earlier question: if God is anticipated as Lord of the future, is He really conceived as Lord of the present? The consideration of this question must serve to determine more closely the peculiar character of Jesus' conception of God.

If the problem is viewed externally, one could say that this is exactly the distinguishing characteristic of the phenomenon of religion—that the combining of belief in omnipotence and in miracle is a part of every living religious faith. The religious man believes confidently in God's omnipotence and universal activity, but he hopes to see miraculous evidences of these in his own life, and rejoices in them. However, the true meaning of the paradox is not yet recognized by this external estimate. The paradox is not based on the psychological processes of the believer, but on the essence of faith itself. Since God is for Jesus not an object of intellectual investigation, his affirmations of faith about God have not the character of universal truths, which are intellectually valid without being grounded in the actual life experience of the believer.

The assertion of God's omnipotence is thus no universally valid proposition, to be applied at will, which may be presupposed as a starting-point for a world view. Rather it affirms first and always that God, the determining Power governing my individual life, can be rightly called omnipotent only if I experience this power in my own life, only if God allows me to realize it as fact, if He reveals to me His omnipotence. But this revelation is always a miracle, that is, always an act of the divine will, which is wholly outside my control. The affirmation of faith, that God is Almighty, is then always dependent upon the insight that I cannot perceive and reckon with this omnipotence as a universally valid fact whenever I please, but only if it pleases God. In the appeal "I believe, help my unbelief," which the father of the sick child addressed to Jesus, this paradox finds clear expression. (Mark 9:24) Thus there exists indeed to the eye of man a dualism, since for him ordinary events veil God from him and he may perceive

God only through a miracle. Nevertheless faith knows that God is almighty—but has this knowledge only because of miracle.

This last statement does not mean that a miracle would prove to a skeptic the fact of the existence of God and His sovereignty. For in that case the assertion of God's sovereignty would be seen as a universal truth which can by logical reasoning be made intelligible to everyone; the miracle would then be regarded as a universally accredited, extraordinary event, from which the conclusion may be drawn that it depends upon a divine cause. On the contrary, miracle *as such* means the activity of God; therefore the understanding of an event as a miracle is not a conclusion from what is perceived, but the perception itself apprehends the miracle. Hence only the faith which arises simultaneously with the sight of the miracle is true faith. Just as little as there can be a belief in omnipotence in general, can there be a belief in miracles in general; that is, events which were for Jesus revelations of the will of God cannot be presented universally as miracles on the basis of which a man should believe. Those into whose lives these events do not come with the faith-creating might of God's activity must obviously regard them not as miracles, but only as astonishing events.

Though in one sense belief in God is the necessary presupposition of belief in miracles, it is not belief in God as an explanation of the phenomena of the world (for the world always hides God, if He does not will to reveal Himself by miracle), but belief as the obedience which is ready to perceive the claim of God upon man in all situations. The doubter, then, who claims to have at his disposal a criterion by which he can prove whether God exists or not, will never see miracles; miracles can be seen only by the doubter who despairs of his own strength and ability to see God if God does not reveal Himself, but who is ready to let God speak to him.

If Jesus' belief in miracles is understood as a general conviction that certain happenings, which we today are accustomed to attribute to natural causes, depend upon a higher, divine cause, then the belief is meaningless and has no relation to his idea of God. But if this belief is understood as the expression of the faith that God's will is not in general visible but reveals itself in special and particular events, then it belongs of necessity to his idea of God. It involves the same paradox which is characteristic of Jesus' whole thought of God: God at once the remote and the near. God is distant, wholly other, in so far as everyday occurrences hide Him from the unbeliever; God is near for the believer who sees His activity.

Moreover, the idea of miracles is a necessary expression of Jesus' thought of God in that it makes plain the opposition of the concept of God to the concept of law. God's act is not the expression of cosmic law, but comes from His free personal will. The belief in miracles denies that the causality of events is a necessity comprehensible by reason; whoever sees an occurrence as a miracle ascribes it directly to the will of God. The idea of miracle, and indeed Jesus' whole thought of God, requires renunciation of the possibility of understanding the world process in the light of universal conformity to law. The concept of miracle, the concept of God in Jesus' sense, does away with the concept of nature.

Whoever affirms Jesus' thought accepts also the paradox that an event which from the observer's viewpoint must be regarded as a natural occurrence, as a part of the world process determined by law, is in reality something different, that is, a direct act of God. When he says "miracle" he suspends the concept of nature, the category of cause and effect, which otherwise dominates his thinking. He knows however that he cannot do this at will, and of himself has no right to do it. For God is the distant God, whom the course of nature hides from his eyes; God is near only for faith, and faith originates only in miracle. The "natural" view of the world is for man the unbelieving view, from which he cannot free himself by his own desire.

5. *Belief in Prayer*

The same paradox appears in the belief of Jesus concerning prayer. Both liturgical and private prayer were highly developed and cultivated in Judaism at the time of Jesus. There is therefore nothing new nor striking in the fact that Jesus and his disciples prayed; the religious Jew had—very probably even in Jesus' time—a prayer which he must say three times a day, the so-called "Eighteen Benedictions." The adherents of John the Baptist had their special prayer, as we know from an allusion in Luke 11:1; similarly the early Christian community had its prayer, the Lord's prayer, which was attributed to Jesus, as the sect of John ascribed their prayer to their master. (Matt. 6:9–13, Luke 11:1–4) How far the Lord's prayer was really formulated by Jesus cannot now be determined; at least it must be characteristic of him.

The oldest wording is no longer ascertainable, since Matthew and Luke differ from each other, and since especially in the case of Luke the different manuscripts diverge sharply from one another. The oldest text of Matthew probably ran:

> "Our Father in heaven,
> hallowed be Thy name,
> Thy Kingdom come,
> Thy will be done
> as in heaven, so on earth.
> Our daily bread give us today,
> and forgive us our debts,
> as we forgive our debtors,
> and lead us not into temptation
> but deliver us from evil."

The oldest text of Luke probably read:

"Father,
hallowed be Thy name,
Thy Kingdom come.
Our daily bread give us daily,
and forgive us our sins,
for we also forgive everyone who has wronged us,
and lead us not into temptation."

The first three petitions (according to the text of Matthew) are presumably all meant in the eschatological sense; that is, they ask that the Kingdom of God may come, that God's name may be made holy, and His will be fulfilled on earth. However, "Hallowed be Thy name" was perhaps added as a liturgical introduction to the prayer. The fourth petition concerns physical life, the fifth, forgiveness of sins. The sixth perhaps means, may God keep the suppliant from falling away in the hour of danger and persecution; if so, this last could scarcely have come from Jesus himself but had its origin in the church.

The unique character of the Lord's prayer as contrasted with Jewish prayers does not consist in any special originality of formulation or content. On the contrary, all the petitions have parallels in Jewish prayers, for the most part in the "Eighteen Benedictions" already mentioned. The Lord's prayer is unique in its great simplicity and brevity, in its lack of pompous invocations and expressions of homage to God, such as are characteristic of the liturgical and literary prayers of the Jews. This simplicity is significant for Jesus' conception of prayer. It shows that *prayer is not thought of as an achievement* for the sake of which God must hear the suppliant. This opinion is expressly repudiated as heathenish: "And when you pray, do not babble like the heathen, for they think they are heard if they use many words." (Matt. 6:7)

Prayer is then not an especially virtuous religious act, of which a man can be proud, contrasting himself with others; it is talking with God, and concerns God alone. (Matt. 6:5–6) It constitutes no claim of the petitioner; it invokes the goodness of God, which can be trusted, for even an earthly father gives good things to his children who ask him—how much more would God do so! (Matt. 7:7–11) But again the goodness of God is not under human control, no universally valid fact on which one can reckon; rather, only he who is willing to accept such goodness as a constituent factor in the reality of his own life and let it dominate his life can assert it, can trust it.

"For if you pardon men their offences,
then your heavenly Father will also pardon you.
But if you do not pardon men,
then your Father will also not pardon you."

(Matt. 6:14–15)

How little the readiness to forgive constitutes a claim to the forgiveness of God is shown by the denial of the supposition that it would be enough to forgive a brother seven times. (Matt. 18:21–22) That means, if forgiveness is to be real, there is no question of commensurable achievements upon which the petitioner depends and bases a claim; the petition for forgiveness must be made by men who wholly renounce all claim. This is illustrated by the parable of the unmerciful servant:

"The Kingdom of Heaven is like a king who wished to settle with his servants. When he began the reckoning, a man who owed ten thousand talents was brought before him. Since he could not pay, his master ordered him to be sold, with wife and child and property. Then the servant fell at his feet and said, Be patient with me and I will pay it all. Then the master of that servant pitied him, let him go, and remitted the debt.

"But when the servant had gone out, he met one of his fellow servants who owed him one hundred pence, and he struck him and choked him and said, Pay what you owe. Then his fellow servant fell at his feet and begged him, Be patient with me and I will pay you. But he would not, and went and threw him in prison until he should pay his debt.

"When his fellow-servants saw that, they were angry and went and told everything to their master. Then the master sent for him and said, You wicked servant, I forgave you your whole debt because you asked me, and ought you not to have had pity on your fellow servant as I had on you? And his master, filled with anger, handed him over to the torturers until he should pay his whole debt. So my heavenly Father will do to every one of you who does not forgive his brother from his heart." (Matt. 18:23–35)

The recorded words of Jesus about prayer deal almost entirely with prayer of petition. His directions for prayer are characteristic.

"Ask, it will be given you,
seek, and you will find,
knock, it will be opened to you.
For he who asks, receives,
and he who seeks, finds,
for him who knocks, it will be opened.
Or who among you will give his son a stone when he asks for bread,
or a serpent when he asks for fish?
If you who are evil know how to give good gifts to your children,
how much more will your Father in heaven give good to those who ask Him?" (Matt. 7:7–11)

Two important parables especially emphasize persistent petition.

"Which of you has a friend? If he comes to him at midnight and says to him, My friend, lend me three loaves, for a friend of mine on a journey has come to me, and I have nothing to offer him—the man within the house will answer, Don't bother me; the door is locked, and my children are in bed with me; I cannot rise and give you bread. I tell you, if he does not rise and give it to him because he is his friend, yet because the other does not go away or stop asking, he will get up and give him what he needs." (Luke 11:5–8)

"But he told them a parable to teach them that they ought to pray continually and not be weary. There was in a city a judge who did not fear God nor trouble himself about man. And in the same city was a widow, who came to him and said, Give me my rights against my opponent. At first he would not, but then he said to himself, Although I do not fear God and trouble myself for no man, yet I will settle this woman's case, because she gives me no rest. Otherwise she will finally come and claw my face." (Luke 18:1-5)

It is doubtful whether the parables apply to all petitions or specifically to the prayer for the coming of the Kingdom; Luke at any rate has interpreted the second parable in the latter sense. But it cannot be doubted that when Jesus urges prayer of petition, *petition is meant in the true sense,* that is, prayer is not to bring the petitioner's will into submission to the unchanging will of God, but prayer is to move God to do something which He otherwise would not do. Of course it does not compel God by any magic force, but it moves Him as one man by his request moves another.

For Jesus the theoretical question of how this is possible does not arise, since for him the thought of God is not limited by the idea of conformity to law. The idea of nature or of conformity to law is excluded in the conception of prayer as in that of miracle. If God's activity is free, obviously He can do *either* this or that, and I can ask Him to do one instead of the other. Events in the world depend, according to Jesus' faith, not on a necessity determined by law but on God's free deed—and this includes future events. Why then should I not be able to make requests of Him? But the question arises whether the conception of God is not thereby impaired. Can such a belief in prayer exist together with the belief in omnipotence? Is God still God, if He is influenced in His action by the prayers of men? Does not he who prays on this assumption destroy the thought of omnipotence?

It is true that *in petition the idea of omnipotence is given up;* but here it again becomes clear that the concept of omnipotence as universal truth, a theoretical dogma, does not belong to Jesus' view of God. To be sure, God is for Jesus almighty, but prayer of petition involves the insight that the concept of omnipotence by no means lies at man's disposal as a way of viewing reality, that man does not in actual fact possess the knowledge of God as the Almighty. For this very reason petition is the proper concern of a man who rightly understands his situation before God; if he wished to give up prayers of petition because of the idea of omnipotence, then he would be arrogating to himself a knowledge of God which he does not possess. If he did really perceive God as almighty, if he could find the fact of the omnipotence of God in his own life, then indeed he would have no occasion for petition. But Jesus knew that this is not the actual situation of man, for whom God the omnipotent is the distant God, who therefore must pray that God may show him His activity.

But a still more difficult problem confronts us: *how is prayer of petition to be reconciled with the thought of*

obedience? How can I pray, and at the same time renounce every claim upon God? However, the renunciation of every claim does not mean resignation or
asceticism, a denying of desires, which while I deny
them remain none the less my deepest wishes. Obedience can be attained only by my confessing my wishes
before God, recounting them to Him, as in prayer of
petition—not indeed presenting them as a claim, but
always accompanied by "Not as I will, but as Thou
wilt." Jesus' faith in God is distinguished from any
sort of asceticism and resignation, for together with the
renunciation of all claim, with obedience, there is the
faith that God is there and acts in my behalf. This man
who prays is full of his own desires, and if he rightly
understands his situation he can do nothing else than
express them in prayer. This excludes the supposition
that man by resigned or ascetic renunciation attains a
position of nearness to God, presents himself before
God as one whose obedience is complete. No, since God
is for man primarily the distant God, man must petition
Him in order to be obedient.

Truly we may ask, who can render obedience? Who
has the faith, while renouncing his own claim, that is,
surrendering his desires to God, at the same time to ask
in faith for the fulfilment of his desires? And we can
understand how the petition of a man who desires to
pray may be silenced, and faith may console itself by
the saying of Paul: "The Spirit helps our weakness.

For we do not know what to pray as we ought. But the
Spirit itself intercedes for us with inexpressible sighs.
And He who searches hearts knows what the way of
the Spirit is." (Rom. 8:26, 27)

Modern interpretations of prayer as an inner reconciliation with fate, a reverent submission to the purpose
of God, are far removed from Jesus; his belief in prayer
involves the paradox of the union of trustful petition
with the will to surrender. Therefore all reflection
about the effect of prayer on the spiritual condition of
the suppliant, which so pleases the modern man, is
lacking here—however true in themselves such reflections may be. Who has spoken more beautifully of the
effect of prayer than Achim von Arnim in the verse:

> "Wir steigen im Gebete
> Zu ihm wie aus dem Tod.
> Sein Hauch, der uns umwehte,
> Tat unserm Herzen not."[1]

But Jesus does not think of this. It is therefore a great
mistake to discuss the prayer life of Jesus, to speak of
him as a praying man, to call him the greatest man of
prayer in history; even historically one has no right to
do this. How a man prayed concerns no other man, not
even the historian. And whoever allows himself to
judge how fervently or deeply Jesus prayed, proves only

[1] "We mount, as if from death
to Him in prayer;
His breath which blows around us
heals our heart's deep need."

that he neither understands nor respects Jesus' conception of prayer. For whoever so judges either sees in prayer merely a psychological phenomenon, which can become the object of interesting analysis, or he arrogates to himself God's own right. For according to Jesus, prayer is talking with God; whoever assumes he can evaluate any prayer presumes to stand in the place of God.

6. Faith

Jesus uses the word "faith" for belief both in miracle and in prayer.

"If you have faith like a grain of mustard seed, you will say to this mountain, Go over there, and it will go." (Matt. 17:20)

To the father of the epileptic boy he says, "Everything is possible to him who has faith." (Mark 9:23) In this sense men are rebuked for their lack of faith or their little faith. (Mark 9:19, Matt. 6:30) On the other hand the word "faith" does not mean for him, as later for Paul and John, the obedience of men under God's redeeming revelation, though this use of the term also enters occasionally into the gospel tradition. (Mark 1:15, Luke 18:8) Although the word faith is not especially prominent in his teaching, yet it is characteristic of his thought of God. For Jesus does not speak of faith in God in general, but only with reference to definite, actual situations.

189

When the author of the Epistle of James says, combating a purely theoretical belief in God, "You believe that God exists? You do well. The demons also believe, and tremble" (James 2:19),—the conception of belief here expressed is not "faith" according to Jesus. This intellectual concept of faith, in which belief in God is part of a world view, a general theoretical conviction of the existence of God, arose in missionary preaching, in which it was necessary to proclaim in contrast to polytheism the belief in *one* God. The heathen were those who do not "know" God. (Gal. 4:8, 1 Thess. 4:5); hence "faith" seemed to be correct knowledge about God. In a Christian book of the second century, the *Shepherd of Hermas,* the first commandment is rendered: "First of all believe that God is *one,* who created and formed all things, who called everything from nothingness into existence, who, Himself incomprehensible, comprehends all in Himself."

In this sense, then, according to which belief in God is part of a world-view and stands in opposition to another world-view, in opposition also to doubt of God's existence, Jesus does not speak of faith. Instead, faith is for him the power, in particular moments of life, to take seriously the conviction of the omnipotence of God; it is the certainty that in such particular moments God's activity is really experienced; it is the conviction that the distant God is really the God near at hand, if

man will only relinquish his usual attitude and be ready
to see the nearness of God. In the sense of Jesus it is
possible to have faith only if one is obedient, and thus
every frivolous misuse of faith in God is excluded.

7. *God the Father*

God who is near is called Father, and men are His
children. Here again it is significant that Jesus does
not intend to teach any new conception of God and does
not announce the fact of man's sonship to God as a
new and unheard-of truth. The view of God as Father
was in fact current in Judaism, and God was addressed
as Father both by the praying congregation and by individuals. Judaism as well as Jesus affirms that a man
may consider himself a son of God when he obeys God's
commands. In the proverbial collection of Ben Sirach
it is said:

"Be a father to orphans
and as a husband to the widows,
then God will call you son,
and be gracious to you and rescue you from destruc-
    tion." (Ecclus. 4:10)

And Jesus says:

"Love your enemies and pray for your persecutors,
that you may be sons of your Father in heaven."
(Matt. 5:45)

The highest that can be said of man, the final word,
is that he is a "son of God." The designation appears

as an eschatological title in Judaism and in words of the Lord. When the 17th Psalm of Solomon describes the rule of the Messiah in the last age in the holy land, we read:

"He knows them, that they are all sons of their God."
(Psalms Sol. 17:30)

And in the Book of Jubilees God promises Israel concerning the time of deliverance:

"They shall do my commandments, and I will be their Father
and they shall be My children.
    And they shall all be called children of the living God, and all angels and all spirits will know and recognize that they are my children and that I am their Father in steadfastness and in righteousness, and that I love them." (Jub. 1:24, 25)

So Jesus' word promises:

    "Blessed are the peace-makers, for they shall be called sons of God." (Matt. 5:9)

and in the saying recorded by Luke concerning those risen from the dead,

    "They are like the angels, and they are sons of God, since they are sons of the resurrection." (Luke 20:36; however the text here is not reliable.)

This mode of expression shows plainly that there is no question of a new conception of God and men presented by Jesus; it also shows plainly Jesus' characteristic idea of God. This becomes clear if we consider that the designation of God as Father is common to many religions and religious world views. The early Stoa had already called God Father, and with the later Stoics this appellation is the typical expression of their piety and of their conception of humanity. And it does indeed serve to express the view that man as a part of the whole divine cosmos is in his nature akin to God and is His son. This is expressly stated as "dogma" (*e.g.*, by Epictetus), and from that are deduced the duties of men which follow from this evaluation, and the security which results if man can trust himself to the providence of his Father. *Man's sonship to God* is thus a universal truth which holds for man as such, which is essential to the idea of man. Sonship to God is man's by nature, and is a truth which holds ideally, which is outside his concrete existence in the here and now.

The opposite is meant by the thought of sonship to God in Judaism and by Jesus. As applied to the nation, it appears often in Jewish literature, although it is not so used by Jesus. The Jews are not by nature children of God because they are human beings, but have become children by God's free choice and by the deeds which He has done for them. When the term is applied to the individual, man is not by nature a son of God, but he can be a son in obedience to God, through God's delivering act. Thus sonship to God is nothing self-evident, natural, which belongs to man as man, of which man needs only to become conscious in order to reap the benefits; rather, sonship to God is a miracle. Man is here seen absolutely differently, not as what he is ideally, outside his concrete life, but precisely as what he is *in* his concrete life, once for all, here and now.

But the possibility of such sonship to God of course exists for all men, and one cannot point to particular men who have the special quality of being sons of God. The Father in heaven cares for all men (Matt. 6: 26, 32), and all men are to turn to Him with their petitions. (Matt. 7:7–11) Here too it holds true that the distant God is at the same time near, and yet for the natural man He is remote; sonship to God is not something which man can claim, on which he can depend. Even in the strange land the prodigal son is his Father's son, and the Father, though distant, is his Father. But in the strange land, the fact that he is a son is a judgment against him, and when he realizes his position, a grief. His sonship gives him no claim; it gives only the hope of the Father's forgiving love, and only forgiveness makes the son once more a son.

"This my son was dead and is again alive, he was lost, and is again found," says the Father. (Luke 15:24)

8. *God the Remote and the Near. Sin and Forgiveness*

In the thought of *forgiveness* must be found the final significance of the paradox of God remote and near. God is the remote God, which means first of all: God is

194

not a part of that world which the thought and activity of man can control. God is the near God, which means first of all: God is the Creator of this world of men, which He governs by His providence. This paradox is understandable because the same apparent contradiction characterizes the life of man; for man has departed from God, but God has come to man.

Man has departed from God; he does not see God's activity in the everyday events of the world; the thought of omnipotence is to him an empty speculation which gains meaning only if he sees God's miracles. And when he takes refuge in prayer to God, he abandons the idea of an omnipotent God and confesses that he cannot perceive God. God is the distant God; that means, man stands in the world alone, without God, given over to fate and death like the prodigal son in the strange land. God is the near God; that can only mean, the very sense of insecurity which characterizes the life of man separated from God arises from the fact that God is seeking man. And that God is seeking man can only mean that God imposes His claim upon him. That man is separated from God, then, evidently means that man does not fulfil this demand of God upon him. The distance of God from man has the same cause as the nearness of God, namely, that man belongs to God, that God imposes a claim upon him. When man fails to hear this demand, he himself transforms God's nearness into remoteness.

The above statements cannot be understood as theoretical reflection on the nature of man; for, like the nearness of God, the demand of God can be affirmed only when it is actually felt. This requirement is not that a man should possess a general knowledge that such a thing as a claim of God upon men exists, but that he himself should hear this demand. Then this attitude of man is not something objective, which lies passive before the gaze of the observer, but it is part of the process of living, which is in motion at every instant. Thus this attitude appears anew at every moment, because in each moment God claims man. But that means that man in his present life stands continually at the crisis of decision. The decisive character of the present moment was made clear above, in the sense that the attitude of man in the present determined his future. But it is precisely because of the claim of God that this is true.

For this demand is not a stage play, but deeply serious; to the man who fails to obey this demand, the future is a condemnation. To him God is the distant God; he is a different man than before. He has not because of this disobedience reached a different level of development, is not passing through a new stage in growth; rather, everything has at once become new for him. Under the judgment of condemnation, he has become a wholly different man, he stands as a sinner

before God. Since he is a sinner, God is remote from
him; and precisely because God is the near God, the
man who does not hear His demand is in His sight a
sinner. Since God is near, no neutrality before Him is
possible, there is no far-off realm in which His claim
would not hold.

Therefore man can never control the world and its
possibilities and find security in it; rather the whole
world stands under the curse of remoteness from God,
and it is a secondary consideration whether a man views
it as a soulless and soul-destroying automaton, or as
the playground of Satan and his hellish hosts. The
world stands under a curse, even if the man does not
recognize it and tries to find his way in the world by
the use of his reason, even if he seeks to understand
it by means of the concepts of God and of omnipotence.
For so long as he is not aware that the present moment
is final, is claimed, constrains to decision, his idea of
God is a phantasm.

Jesus does not discuss how large a proportion of
mankind is sinful; he evolves no theory that all are sinners, no theory of original sin. For sin is something
condemned by God in the concrete present moment, not
a universal attribute of human nature theoretically understood apart from time. Sin no more than God can
be discussed in general propositions; otherwise I should
be able to distinguish myself from my sin, whereas in

reality I am myself the sinner. Sin is not a sort of appendage to man; it is the characteristic of sinful humanity. Hence Jesus does not preach that all are sinners, but speaks to sinful men.

Further, he does not discuss the *nature of sin,* since this is for him and his hearers a self-evident proposition, corresponding to the Jewish thought of God which Jesus shares. Sin is the character which belongs inevitably to the man remote from God who denies the claim of God. Since the thought of God's claim and of decision is more radically conceived by Jesus than it is in Judaism, his concept of sin is also more radical.

Because the crisis of decision in the present moment gives man his essential character, he cannot console or justify himself by viewing his sin as a weakness which forms no part of his true nature, or as a mistake which is an exception to be outweighed by appealing to his normal self. For since the whole man is compelled to decision, the whole man is here at stake, and determines by his choice his whole future. Nor can man in the face of the call to repentance point to his ideal self which lies outside the realm of empirical fact. His sins do not mark a stage in his moral development, nor are they a condition which in a sense provides material for further moral progress, nor something which he ought to and can overcome (*he,* after all, is the sinner!) ; but it is the position in which he is wholly involved, so that he cannot by virtue of a "better self" escape from it.

He stands before God as a sinner, that is, his sin has not relative but absolute character; he is condemned, and can appeal to nothing which he has been or has achieved. And at this point the deeper radicalism of Jesus compared to Judaism becomes evident; for Judaism still assumed the value of human achievement or at least allowed the repentance of man to have value as a quality which recommended him to God.

If there is any help for man who is a sinner, it can only be the forgiveness of God. Jesus proclaims the forgiveness of God, and here also he does not proclaim anything new to Judaism. For what consolation does the Jewish prayer of penitence offer, except the grace of God who forgives sins? "Praise to Thee, Lord, who freely forgives," says the Jew in his daily prayer. However, in the message of Jesus the more radical thought of God's grace and forgiveness corresponds to the more radical concept of sin. In Judaism God overlooks the sins of the religious, and this is God's grace; God condemns the completely sinful and godless, and therefore the religious man feels himself fundamentally good. He can point, if not to his good works, at least to his humble confession of sin, and therefore appeal to God's grace. Thus the seer in 4 Ezra not only mentions the first possibility—

"For the righteous, who have laid up many good works
   before Thee,
will receive reward for their works." (4 Ezra 8:33)—

but also, with even more emphasis, he says:

"For in truth there is none born of women who sins
    not,
not one of those who have lived, who has not trans-
    gressed;
then indeed are Thy justice and Thy kindness manifest,
    O Lord,
when Thou pitiest those who have no treasure of good
    works." (4 Ezra 8:31–36)

And consistently he hears the angel answer:

"You have often reckoned yourself with the sinners.
Do so no more. You will receive more praise from the
Most High because, as is fitting, you are humble and do
not count yourself with the righteous. Therefore you
shall have so much greater honor." (4 Ezra 8:47–49)

To rebuke men who think they have something to
depend upon before God, Jesus told the tale of the
Pharisee and the tax-collector.

"Two men went up to the temple to pray, the one a
Pharisee, the other a tax-collector. The Pharisee stood
up and prayed, God, I thank Thee that I am not like
other men, robbers, evil doers, adulterers, or even like
this tax-collector. I fast twice a week and give a tenth
of all I have. But the tax-collector stood at a distance,
would not even raise his eyes, but beat his breast and
said, God be merciful to me, a sinner. I tell you, he
went home justified rather than the other." (Luke 18:
10–14)

The Pharisee was not condemned because he spoke
falsely in what he said; but the fact that he compared
himself with others, that he desired to exhibit his virtue

before God, showed that he did not rightly understand what God's grace meant. For God's grace can be known only when a man realizes his utter helplessness, and perceives nothing more in himself to which he can appeal. The Pharisee also did not understand God's demand, else he would have known that this left him no surplus time to do some special deed which would give him an advantage over other men; that a man can never do more than is required of him.

"So you must say, when you have done all that was
    ordered,
We are servants, we have done only our proper work."
                                    (Luke 17:10)

Only when the requirement of obedience is wholly grasped can *the thought of grace and of forgiveness* be wholly understood; and the message of forgiveness then appears in its unity with the call to repentance. Forgiveness does not mean that the sin is to be compensated for (the man is *wholly* disobedient); it can only be *forgiven.* When a man accepts forgiveness, he condemns himself most severely, he really bows his head under the judgment of God. And as his character as sinner signified that he failed in the decision and became another man, a condemned man who had lost his freedom, so forgiveness means that he is to become a new man through God's grace, that he has his freedom once more, that God does not abandon His claim upon him but also does not deprive him of His grace—that

God means to bring him out of remoteness into nearness to Himself.

What happens in forgiveness may be understood by considering the meaning of forgiveness in the relationship between two men who love each other. If a man has offended another, not to say wronged him, nothing can restore him to the old relationship except the forgiveness of the other. And this forgiveness cannot rest on any thought of compensation, as if there were still so much that is good and valuable in the offender that the other could overlook the mistake. For by the offense the relationship is *wholly* destroyed, and the one becomes to the other entirely a stranger. The love which once existed depended—if it was genuine—not on certain attractive qualities, but embraced the whole man. And the whole man now stands, since he did not meet the crisis, before the other as a different man, and all his attractive qualities and his possibilities of development do not help him at all. Only one thing can help him—if something new happens, if his friend has the strength to forgive him and thereby make him a new man. If something new happens—that means, that forgiveness is not a necessary result determined by the nature of the man who forgives, something upon which the offender can count (if he did, he would obviously be unworthy of it) ; but it is an act arising wholly from the free good will of a person, wholly a gift.

In the same way God's forgiveness is real forgiveness only if it is His free act, an event. Man can assert it only if he experiences it as an event in time, even as sin is an event. He cannot assume it, nor can he deduce it from a conception of God. Thus it is clear that Jesus in this connection too does not preach a new idea of God—as if God had hitherto been represented as too arbitrary and hard, vindictive and angry, and was rather to be thought of as benevolent and gracious. On the contrary. The Jews knew that God is a gracious God as well as a God who is angry with the sinner, so far as it can be known through the possession of an intellectual concept of God. And no one has spoken more forcibly of the wrath of God (although without using the word) than Jesus, precisely because he proclaims God's grace. Because he conceives radically the idea of the grace of God, he makes it plain that God's forgiveness must be for man an event in time, that the relation of "I" and "Thou" exists between God and man, that God stands opposite to man as another Person over whom the man can have no sort of control, who meets man with His claim and with His grace, whose forgiveness is pure gift.

This is the reason that the preaching of Jesus is addressed first of all to the poor and sinful, and that he allowed himself to be blamed as the friend of tax-collectors and sinners.

"The gospel of deliverance is proclaimed to the poor."
(Matt. 11:5)

"Blessed are you poor, for yours is the Kingdom of God." (Luke 6:20)

For such perceive God's claim more clearly than the respectable people, and also know better how to accept a free gift. A whole series of comparisons and parables illustrates this fact.

"But how do you judge? A man had two sons; he went to the first and said, My son, go today and work in my vineyard. He answered, Yes, sir, and did not go. Then the man went to his second son and said the same to him. But he said, I will not go. Then he thought better of it and went. Which of the two obeyed his father? They said, The second. Then Jesus said, Truly I tell you, tax-collectors and prostitutes will enter the Kingdom of God before you." (Matt. 21 : 28–31)

"Who of you who has a hundred sheep, and has lost one of them, does not leave the ninety-nine in the pasture and go after the lost one until he finds it? When he has found it, he joyfully puts it on his shoulder; and when he comes home he calls his friends and neighbors together and says, Be glad with me, for I have found my lost sheep again. I tell you, so there will be more joy in heaven over one sinner who repents than over ninety-nine righteous people who need no repentance.

"Or if a woman has ten pieces of silver and has lost one, does she not light a lamp and clean the house, and seek carefully until she finds it? and when she has found it she calls her friends and neighbors together and says, Be glad with me, for I have found my lost silver piece. So I tell you, there will be joy among the angels of God over one sinner who repents." (Luke 15:4–10)

"A man had two sons, and the younger of them said to his father, Give me my share of the property. And he gave him his share of the whole. Not long after, the younger took all that he had and went into a distant land, and there spent his money in luxurious living. And when he had wasted it all, there was a severe famine in that land, and he began to suffer from hunger. Then he went and attached himself to one of the citizens, who sent him into the fields to herd his swine. And he tried to satisfy his hunger with the husks which the swine ate, and no one gave him anything. Then he came to himself, and said, How many of my father's hired servants have more than enough bread, while I am dying here of hunger. I will arise and go to my father and say to him, Father, I have sinned against heaven and against you. I am no longer worthy to be called your son; make me one of your hired servants. And he rose and went to his father.

"But when he was still far off, his father saw him and pitied him, and ran and fell on his neck and kissed him. Then his son said to him, Father, I have sinned against heaven and against you; I am no longer worthy to be called your son. But the father said to his servants, Quick, bring the best coat and put it on him, and put a ring on his hand and shoes on his feet. And bring the fatted calf and kill it, for we will have a feast. For my son here was dead and is again alive, he was lost, and is again found. And they began to feast.

"But his oldest son was in the field. When he came back and reached the house, he heard music and dancing. Then he called one of the servants and asked him what it meant. He told him, Your brother has come, and your father has killed the fatted calf because he has him safe again. Then he was angry and would not go in. His father however came out and urged him.

But he answered his father, Think how many years I have served you, and I have not disobeyed your orders, but you never gave me a kid so that I could have a feast with my friends, and now when your son comes, who wasted your property with prostitutes, you kill the fatted calf for him. But he said to him, My son, you are always with me, all that is mine is yours. But we must rejoice and feast, for your brother here was dead and is again alive, he was lost and is again found." (Luke 15:11–32)

All these words are directed against those who cannot realize what God's grace and forgiveness are, who do not understand that man can receive God's goodness only as a gift, and that therefore it is really only the sinner who knows what grace is. Finally, this is why children can serve as an example. They do not yet know what achievements and claims are, and they can accept free gifts.

"And children were brought to him, for him to lay his hands on them; but his followers rebuked them. When Jesus saw that, he was indignant, and said to them, Let the children come to me; forbid them not; for to such belongs the Kingdom of God. I tell you truly, he who does not accept the Kingdom of God like a child will never come into it. And when he laid his hand upon them, he put his arms around them." (Mark 10:13–16)

Now it may be asked, if God thus meets man as a "Thou," is He not conceived as a person? Are not all these ideas of God and man meaningless, since they depend upon a personal conception of God? For how can God be thought of as a person? Is this not naïve anthropomorphism? Indeed all these ideas do become without meaning if the human person, the "I," who is first of all concerned, is looked at from without, if the "I" is described as one can describe in general propositions the nature of a human being; if, as usually results, the individual man is regarded as a specimen of the genus *homo*. In that case of course God as personal also must appear as such a specimen, perhaps somewhat greater and more spiritual, above all "invisible"; then God would indeed be a "gaseous vertebrate," as has been satirically said.

In the thought of Jesus, however, man is not seen in this way from outside, thus himself acting as observer; instead, the observer's standpoint is abandoned. Man is seen in his essential being, in his life, which is lived in specific decisive moments in the present, which cannot be understood through a general description of humanity. A man has no control in his ideas over this essential self, for he cannot stand to one side and observe it, he *is* it. Obviously no one can prove to a man that he has this essential life, because for this proof the observer's standpoint would be necessary. But a man can know that in this actual life of his he is confronted and claimed by a "Thou." Indeed it is in reality only this claim which gives him his life as a self. And that he, "coming to himself," knows himself to be claimed by an inescapable "Thou," means that he knows of God, and of God as a Person who speaks to him as "thou." He can therefore regard God no more than himself from an observer's standpoint, and the reproach of anthropomorphism has lost its terrors for him.

This understanding of God and His forgiveness shows conclusively how far Jesus stands from all humanistic idealism, according to which the concept of sin in the real sense does not exist. Humanism knows merely the development of humanity with its possibilities and its different stages; here the true value of man is the ideal self, which is beyond his concrete empirical existence, and because of which no man can be wholly lost. Love is a universal love of mankind, so that individuals may be ignored and humanity may be made happy through institutions.

It is clear that belief in forgiveness presupposes a God who acts as a person and whose act of mercy is an event in time. Thus it is a wholly false supposition that Jesus' belief concerning God marks an especially high level in humanity's developing consciousness of God, that to him—as some one has expressed it—God became the "representation of the ought-to-be as the power of love." In this view, when the primitive idea of God, which was based on the personification of powers of nature, vanishes gradually behind the infinitude of the causal sequence, the concept of God gains in coherence and consistency in proportion as it achieves a firm position in connection with the claims and needs of the human spirit, and becomes the "irreduceable co-efficient of the achievement of moral processes in self-consciousness." Jesus—so it is thought—completed the decisive modification in the concept of God from the personified power of nature, the power over what *is,* to the "representation of the ought-to-be as the power of love."

Whoever speaks in this way, however he may desire to honor Jesus, has not understood him. First of all, he has not understood that he himself, according to Jesus, is claimed by God, an authority experienced as external to himself, and is by Him constrained to decision in the present moment—that God requires from him obedience. Instead of the Power whom man obeys and for whom he decides, he knows only the law of his own spiritual being, and the idea of God becomes "the irreduceable coefficient of moral processes in self-consciousness." Thus he can no longer think of God as the Power over what is (as Jesus conceived Him), but only as the Power over what ought to be, that is, only the personification of what the law of his own being demands of him. Then at the moment of claimed or rendered obedience, the demand is actually made by the man himself, the true ideal man, who by his autonomy establishes himself and his own value. Jesus knows no such ideal man; he has before his eyes the actual concrete man as he stands before God. Otherwise the assertion of the love and forgiveness of God is meaningless, for in Jesus' thought love and forgiveness are not ideas but are real events in the life in time of concrete men.

Both sin and forgiveness are *temporal events in the life of men.* Thus, even though all men are sinners before God, sin is not a universal characteristic of the existence of man or of human nature such as corporeality, nor is it some magical or mysterious quality of the sinner. Jesus does not recognize any evil *nature;* he regards as evil only the evil *will* of the disobedient man. Therefore the grace of forgiveness is not the infusion into the sinner of a higher nature which in some magical or mysterious way transforms him. However remote the sinner is from grace, and however great the transformation to be effected by forgiveness, yet pardon is for him the most comprehensible thing in the world, as easy to understand as a word of love and pardon between man and man, without being in the least something to take for granted.

Just as God does not mean to Jesus a higher nature to be enjoyed in the sacrament, God's forgiveness also is no sacramental grace but a personal act of God. Then it is also plain that the experience of grace and of the forgiveness of God, which destroys the old man and creates the new, does not transfer man to a higher plane, either where he can passively enjoy his new nature or where he must guard it with anxious care through asceticism. Rather, grace holds fast the demand for obedience, since real forgiveness condemns disobedience. Whoever then becomes a new man through forgiveness is reborn to obedience. If any one thinks he has received forgiveness, without becoming conscious of God's will in his own life, such forgiveness is illusory, as the parable of the unmerciful servant shows. (Matt. 18:23–35)

Thus it has finally become clear in what sense God is for Jesus God of the present and of the future. God is God of the present, because His claim confronts man in the present moment, and He is at the same time God of the future, because He gives man freedom for the present instant of decision, and sets before him as the future which is opened to him by his decision, condemnation or mercy. God is God of the present for the sinner precisely because He casts him into remoteness from Himself, and He is at the same time God of the future because He never relinquishes His claim on the sinner and opens to him by forgiveness a new future for new obedience.

The less the grace of God is assumed to be an essential quality of Deity on which man can depend, and the more it is understood as becoming effective only in the act of forgiveness to the individual man, so much more urgent must be the question, *when and how man gains the right to speak of forgiveness.* The act of forgiveness! Is there any such act? Is there a criterion to determine when it occurs, how it is accomplished, so that a man may become sure of forgiveness? Obviously not a subjective spiritual experience can be meant; there can be in question only an event which confronts man, which happens to him from without; an event which manifests itself as an act of God, because it confronts a man as authority. It presents the claim of God to him and thus it identifies the forgiveness as divine, because it is pure gift, delivering man while judging him.

Again, this event which comes to the man cannot be an occurrence to be looked at objectively, a part of the world of objects constituting man's environment, which can be observed and analyzed in order to establish the fact that it is the event of forgiveness, to which the man can now relate himself. For the act of forgiveness between God and man, as between man and man, escapes observation. The act of forgiveness does not occur in empty space; it is real only in its reference to the particular man. Therefore only he who is forgiven knows the act of forgiveness.

What more can be said of this act of forgiveness? The tradition of the church has rightly held fast to the fact that forgiveness is an event, and speaks in this sense of the *acts of salvation*. The only question is whether the church has understood the event in the same sense as Jesus. It sees the event, the decisive act of deliverance, in the death of Jesus, or in his death and resurrection. In this the church is wrong, so far as the death and resurrection of Jesus are understood merely as given facts of history which may be determined and established by evidence. As soon as the observer's standpoint toward the event is taken, it is no longer the event of forgiveness—for that can never be experienced by an observer. Therefore all speculations and theories are false which seek to establish by proofs that the death and resurrection of Jesus have the power of forgiveness and atonement for sin. If the death and resurrection of Jesus are asserted as redemptive acts, in the sense of cosmic events which affect mankind in general so that the individual can rely upon them, this is not the meaning of Jesus—neither sin nor forgiveness is really taken seriously. Not sin, for it is thought of as a universal human attribute; nor forgiveness, for it is conceived as a mere event in the world of external objects, on which man by his very theories and proofs exercises judgment, asserting that divine forgiveness can and must be thus and so.

Moreover, Jesus did not speak of his death and resurrection and their redemptive significance. Some sayings of such a character are indeed attributed to him in the gospels, but they originated in the faith of the church —and none of them even in the primitive church, but in Hellenistic Christianity. The two most important of these sayings are the words concerning "ransom" and those spoken at the Lord's supper.

"The Son of man came not to be served, but to serve, and to give his life as ransom for many." (Mark 10:45)

"When they ate, he took the bread, said the blessing, and broke it, gave it to them and said, Take it, this is my body.

"And he took the cup, gave thanks, and gave it to them, and they all drank from it. And he said to them, This is my blood of the covenant, which is shed for many." (Mark 14:22–24)

The first of these sayings is a Hellenistic variation of an older saying, which Luke has preserved:

"Who is greater, he who sits at table or he who serves? You say, he who sits at table? But I am among you as one who serves." (Luke 22:27)

The words concerning the Lord's supper are liturgical formulations from the Hellenistic celebration of the Eucharist, replacing an older account, of which traces still remain, especially in Luke.

It is then certain that Jesus did not speak of his death and resurrection as redemptive acts. This would not prevent others from so speaking of them, if they mean events in which *they* become aware of the divine forgiveness. Just as it cannot be determined that any events of history—including the cross of Jesus—manifest "objectively" the divine forgiveness, so it is impossible to prove on objective grounds that they may not do so. In both cases a man would assume to possess the criterion of how the event of divine forgiveness must appear. If the event of forgiveness is a happening in time which comes to a man from without, yet is not an observable process which can be objectively demonstrated, then there remains only to inquire how the character of this event in the sense of Jesus can be more clearly defined.

Jesus does not point to any way which can be universally recognized, in which a man becomes conscious of the forgiveness of God—he simply proclaims this forgiveness. The event is nothing else than *his word,* as it confronts the hearer. For the truth of his word he offers no evidence whatever, neither in his miracles, the significance of which is not to accredit his words (for he expressly repudiates attestation through miracles (Mark 8:11, 12)), nor in his personal qualities, which apparently aroused in his contemporaries antagonism rather than faith. If he had for some men a certain fascination, this may rather have tended to distract attention from the content of his words; and certainly there is no mention of this in the record.

Also neither in his sayings nor in the records of the primitive church is there any mention of his metaphysical nature. The primitive community did indeed believe him to be the Messiah, but it did not ascribe to him a particular metaphysical nature which gave his words authority. On the contrary, it was on the ground of the authority of his words that the church confessed that God had made him Lord of the church. Greek Christianity soon represented Jesus as Son of God in the sense of ascribing a divine "nature" to him, and thus introduced a view of his person as far removed as possible from his own.

Equally foreign to him is the modern view of him as a *"personality."* He would by no means have understood, and would certainly never have approved, the tendency to regard his personal power of faith, his enthusiasm, his heroism, and his readiness for sacrifice as attestation of the truth of his word. For all these are human traits, and are included in the realm of human possibilities and human judgment. And no amount of energy and sacrificial courage can ever prove anything concerning the truth of the cause which a hero represents. The view of Jesus as a great character or a hero is simply the opposite of Jesus' conception of man; for man as a "character" has his centre in himself, and the hero relies on himself; in this the greatness of the man consists; this is the æsthetic point of view. Jesus however sees man in his relation to God, under the claim of God.

There is indeed one estimate of him which is consistent with his own view, the estimate of him not as a personality, but as one sent by God, as bearer of the word. In this sense he says:

"Blessed is he who finds no cause of offense in me."
(Matt. 11:6)

"Whoever acknowledges me before men,
him will the Son of Man also acknowledge before the
     angels of God.
Whoever denies me before men,
will be denied before the angels of God."
(Luke 12:8, 9)

Perhaps the form in which Mark preserves this last saying is older; at least it shows clearly what the early tradition regarded as the significance of the person of Jesus.

"Whoever is ashamed of me *and of my words* in this
     adulterous and sinful generation,
of him the Son of Man will be ashamed, when he comes
     in the glory of his Father with the holy angels."
(Mark 8:38)

Jesus is therefore the bearer of the word, and in the word he assures man of the forgiveness of God.

That this word can be the event of divine forgiveness will indeed be understood only if we set ourselves free from a commonly held modern view-point which has had a fatal influence on historical study. This is the habit of understanding the word only as the natural self-expression of the speaking individual. It then makes little difference whether this individual is seen æsthetically or idealistically as personality, character, "form" (Gestalt), or the like; or naturalistically in the light of evolution as the exponent of a particular historical or cultural situation. From these view-points, a word can no longer be in the real sense an "event" for the hearer; for by means of correct analysis he can have in view beforehand all the possibilities of what may be said to him.

But if we return to the real significance of "word," implying as it does a relationship between speaker and hearer, then the word can become an event to the hearer, because it brings him into this relationship. But this presupposes ultimately a wholly different conception of man, namely that the possibilities for man and humanity are not marked out from the beginning and determined in the concrete situation by character or circumstances; rather, that they stand open, that in every concrete situation new possibilities appear, that human life throughout is characterized by successive decisions. Man is constrained to decision by the word which brings a new element into his situation, and the word therefore becomes to him an event; for it to become an event, the hearer is essential.

Therefore the attestation of the truth of the word lies wholly in what takes place between word and hearer. This can be called subjective only by him who either has not understood or has not taken seriously the meaning of "word." Whoever understands it and takes it seriously knows that there is no other possibility of God's forgiveness becoming real for man than the word. In the word, and not otherwise, does Jesus bring forgiveness. Whether his word is truth, whether he is sent from God—that is the decision to which the hearer is constrained, and the word of Jesus remains: "Blessed is he who finds no cause of offense in me."

INDEX OF BIBLICAL QUOTATIONS

INDEX OF BIBLICAL QUOTATIONS

Topical Index

224

TOPICAL INDEX

Good works (human achievement),
51, 70 f., 78, 80 f., 99 f., 146 ff.,
152, 182, 199 ff., 206

Greek thought, 68, 72, 101, 103,
119 f., 133 f., 138, 158, 168, 170

Hellenistic Christianity, 12 f., 63,
108, 126, 153, 213 f., 216
Judaism, 67

History, 3–11, Ch. I, 106, 140, 188,
213 f.

Human achievement, *see* Good
works

Humanism, 46, 52 ff., 68, 72, 80,
84 f., 87, 108, 111–114, 116, 136,
193, 208 f.

Ideal, idealism, ideal man, 10 f.,
18, 35, 38, 52 ff., 56, 68, 72, 79,
84 f., 87, 93, 98 f., 101, 103 f.,
107, 111 ff., 116, 119, 130, 133,
136, 193, 198, 208 f., 218

Individualism, 47 f., 52 f., 84, 105,
119, 153 f., 217 f.

Interim-ethic, 107, 127 ff.

James, Epistle of, 190

Jewish religion, Ch. I, § 1, 49,
Ch. III, §§ 2 and 3, 78, 89, 91 f.,
111, 125, 127, Ch. IV, § 1, 150,
155 f., 158 f., 161 ff., 166 ff., 172,
180 ff., 191 ff., 198 ff., 203

John, Gospel of, 12, 152, 189

John the Baptist, Ch. I, § 3, 45,
49, 57 f., 100, 152, 180

Kierkegaard, 31, 115 f.

Kingdom of God, 22, 24, Ch. II,
107 f., Ch. III, § 8, 140, 152 f.,
155 f., 158 f., 173, 181, 185

Law, cosmic, natural, 6, 133 ff.,
140, 151, 163 f., 168, 171, 174,
178 f., 185

Law, Jewish, Ch. I, § 1, 44, 58,
Ch. III, §§ 2 and 3, 74 ff., 81 f.,
91 f., 111, 121 f., 125 f., 136

Lord's Prayer, 42, 155, 180 f.

Lord's Supper, 29, 39, 153, 214

Love of God, 58, 79, 153 f., 194,
202, 208 ff.
of neighbor, 58, 69, 79, 91, 94,
Ch. III, § 7

Mandæans, 24

Marriage, 62, 91, 99 f., 104 f., 127,
129

Messiah, Messianic hope,
Jesus, 9, 26, 28 f., 38 f., 52, 64,
123–126, 174, 215 f.
Jewish, 19, Ch. I, §§ 2 and 3,
38–41, 52, 107, 192*l*

Miracle, miraculous (supernatural), 22, 36 ff., 46, Ch. IV, § 4,
185, 189, 194, 195, 215

Monotheism, 138 f., 190

Mysticism, 47 f., 153 ff.

Nationalism of Jesus, 43–47, 106 ff.
Jewish, 19, 41 f., 65 f., 193

Nature, 3, 36, 50, 102 f., 137, 151
f., 162 f., 166, 169, 172, 179, 185,
193, 208 ff., 215 f.

Nazarene, 24

Obedience, 17 ff., 48, Ch. III,
§§ 3–4, 91 f., 101 f., 109, 112 ff.,
117 ff., 121 f., 127, 129, 136, 146,
154 f., 171, 178, 187, 189, 191,
193, 196, 209, 211

Palestinian tradition, *see* Aramaic
tradition

Pantheism, 134, 154, 162, 172

Parables, 31 ff., 36 f., 38, 53 f., 58,
73 f., 79, 94 f., 96, 104, 183 ff.,
194, 200, 203–206, 211

Paul, 62 f., 111, 126, 187, 189 f.

Perfection, 120, 121, 126

Personality (character), 47, 52, 68,
84, 105, 119, 130, 153, 218
of Jesus, 8 ff., 12, 13, 123, 130,
215 ff.

Pharisees, 20, 21, 69, 200 f.

Plato, 11

Political, politics, 19, 22, 25, 42 f.,
106 ff.

Prayer, 42, 64, 71, 81, 143, 146 f.,
155, Ch. IV, § 5, 189, 195